KU-362-125

REFORMATION MYTHS

FIVE CENTURIES
OF MISCONCEPTIONS
AND MISFORTUNES
(SOME)

RODNEY STARK

First published in Great Britain in 2017

Society for Promoting Christian Knowledge
36 Causton Street
London SW1P 4ST
www.spck.org.uk

British Library Cataloguing-in-Publication Data
A catalogue record for this book is available from the British Library

ISBN 978–0–281–07827–1
eBook ISBN 978–0–281–07828–8

1 3 5 7 9 10 8 6 4 2

Typeset by Manila Typesetting Company
Printed in Great Britain by Ashford Colour Press

eBook by Manila Typesetting Company

Produced on paper from sustainable forests

Contents

Introduction
The mythical 'Protestant'

The date of 31 October 2017 is the 500th anniversary of Martin Luther's nailing his *Ninety-five Theses* to the door of the Castle Church in Wittenberg, thereby initiating what became known as the Protestant Reformation. Throughout the year, hundreds of scholarly conferences celebrating the event are being held in all the leading Protestant nations, and even those with Catholic participants will express profound admiration for the many ways in which the Reformation played a major role in the creation of the modern West.

However, an embarrassing question that must be answered at any celebration of the Reformation is: which one do you mean? Three successful Reformations, plus outbursts of Anabaptism, occurred during the sixteenth century (ignoring recent claims that there was a whole series of English Reformations).[1] The only common feature of the three successful Reformations was their rejection of papal authority; otherwise they were quite at odds. Luther's most important theological claim was that salvation comes through faith alone. John Calvin taught that salvation cannot be achieved by any means, but is conferred by God for unknown reasons upon only a chosen few. And Henry VIII's English Reformation conformed to the Roman Catholic position that salvation can be achieved through works as well as faith.

Bitter hatreds also separated these three Reformations. The Lutherans formed monopoly state churches and prohibited all other faiths, subsequently hunting down 'crypto-Calvinists' and burning some of them in Saxony during the 1580s.[2] They also were hostile to 'any people suspected of Anabaptism or of abusing the holy sacraments by practicing Zwinglianism'.[3] The Calvinists permitted no 'heresy' in Geneva, and persecuted violators. As for Henry VIII, he not only beheaded some Catholic prelates; he also burned a number of Lutherans, Calvinists, Anabaptists and other 'heretics'.

Consequently, the many celebrations held during 2017 can hardly be in honour of *the* Reformation. Nor does it seem likely that the celebrants are united in honouring the Lutheran Reformation, let alone the English Reformation. The only plausible common basis for all these events is to celebrate the rise of Protestantism. This raises an even more important matter: that so many of the achievements attributed to Protestantism are entirely mythical and some of the actual results of the rise of Protestantism were quite unfortunate. Thus, there will be frequent tributes incorrectly paid to the myths that Protestantism enabled the rise of science and created capitalism. For partisan reasons, much less is apt to be said about the equally mythical claims that Protestantism spurred the rise of individualism and its presumed consequences or that Protestantism has led to secularization. And very little probably will be said about the need for 'priest holes' in many English manor houses, or about laws requiring regular church attendance in England and northern Europe. As for Luther's legacy of violent anti-Semitism, it probably will not be mentioned.

There is an additional and compelling question that probably also will go unaddressed: what is a Protestant? In this brief Introduction I will demonstrate that the category 'Protestant' includes so much variation on such important matters as to be essentially meaningless, except when used very narrowly.

The name Protestant originated with a letter from German princes in 1529 'protesting' against a decision by the emperor to revoke the edict allowing individual princes to choose whether or not to embrace Lutheranism. The word derives either from the Latin *pro* (for) and *testari* (witness) or from *protestatio* (declare). Ironically, perhaps, it was the Vatican that first used the word Protestant 'to lump together . . . a group of loosely interconnected but ultimately distinct movements'.[4] Today, the standard dictionary definition is vague and negative: 'a Protestant is any Christian who is not a Roman Catholic or an Eastern Orthodox Catholic'. Some dictionaries also exclude Anglicans. Nowhere is there a positive definition such as 'a Protestant is one who . . .' The reason for this is simply that it is impossible to list a set of beliefs held in common by all who are called Protestants, or to discover any other feature held in common. Even from earliest days this was true. About all that Lutherans, Calvinists, Anglicans and Anabaptists agreed upon was the divinity of Jesus and the wickedness of the pope.

Thousands of 'Protestant' denominations

If, even in Luther's time, the word Protestant lacked any coherent theological or organizational meaning, consider that since then, 'Protestants' have splintered into approximately 33,000 independent denominations worldwide, according to the 2001 edition of the *World Christian Encyclopedia*. Perhaps as many as 11,000 Protestant denominations are in sub-Saharan Africa alone. Great Britain has more than 500 independent Protestant denominations, ranging from the huge Church of England to small evangelical groups. And there are more than a thousand independent Protestant denominations in the United States, 23 of them having more than a million members each. In his magisterial *Encyclopedia of American Religions* (9th edition), J. Gordon Melton identifies ten major Protestant 'families'. These are clusters of denominations sharing common roots and some degree of theological similarity. Nevertheless, there are immense differences both in theology and in cultural outlook not only across these families, but also *within* them. Consider these two examples.

The Lutheran Family. Even though there has been a recent merger of a number of once-independent ethnic Lutheran denominations (German, Swedish, Danish, etc.), there remain 33 separate Lutheran denominations in the United States. Some of these are very large – the Evangelical Lutherans have nearly 5 million members and the Missouri Lutherans have nearly 3 million. Some are very small – the Lutheran Churches of the Reformation has only about 1,000 members in 15 congregations. There is an amazing degree of theological variation within this 'family'. The Evangelical Lutherans are very liberal; the Missouri Lutherans are very conservative.

The Reformed–Presbyterian Family. Here are the many variations on Calvinism, including the Puritans who founded the Massachusetts Bay Colony. Melton identifies 44 independent denominations within this group. Some of them are tiny, some of them very large – the Presbyterian Church USA has more than 2 million members and the United Church of Christ has more than a million. Both of these large denominations are very liberal theologically, but many of the other groups in the family are extremely conservative. For example, John Calvin probably would feel quite comfortable within the Christian Reformed Church in North America, having more than 300,000 members.

The primary fact is that the 'average' Protestant is a statistical fiction, as has been clear since the very first surveys of religious belief were conducted. Table I.1 is based on a survey of American church members conducted in 1963. Reading down the columns, it is obvious that in some major denominations few believed in these traditional Christian doctrines; in some other major bodies, nearly everyone believed.

Table I.1   Denomination and religious beliefs in the USA in 1963

Denomination	Belief in (percentage)		
	Virgin birth	Second coming	Devil
Congregational*	21	13	6
Methodist	34	21	13
Episcopal	39	24	17
Disciples of Christ	62	36	18
Presbyterian	57	43	31
American Lutheran	66	54	49
American Baptist	69	57	49
Missouri Lutheran	97	75	77
Southern Baptist	99	94	92
Various Evangelical Groups	96	89	90
Total Protestant	**57**	**44**	**38**
Roman Catholic	**81**	**47**	**66**

* Now the United Church of Christ.
Source: Stark and Glock, 1968.

Despite these findings, which have been well known for nearly 50 years and have been replicated many times since, when I recently searched JSTOR for the word 'Protestant' in the title of published social science papers, I obtained 52,522 results, and JSTOR does not include many of the major journals. Here are a few of these titles:

Protestant–Catholic Differences in Educational Achievement.

Catholic/Protestant Differences in Marital Status.

Church and Culture: Protestant and Catholic Modernities.

One could demonstrate the absurdity of these under-takings by revealing that there is at least as much, and probably much more, variation on these matters *among* the Protestants of various types included in these merged 'Protestant' groups, than between the 'average' Protestants and the Catholics – as we saw in Table I.1. Hence, all such reported Protestant–Catholic comparisons are nonsense.

Of course, sometimes the word Protestant can be used meaningfully. Fully in keeping with the current dictionary definition, it sometimes is useful to distinguish Christians who accept the pope's authority from those who don't. For example, using the term 'Protestant nation' to distinguish Denmark from France is legitimate and useful, so long as one remains aware of the remarkable religious diversity entailed by that identification. In any event, in the remain-der of the book I will challenge claims about the meaning-fulness of using the term 'Protestant' to identify a coherent religious outlook.

Let me acknowledge that, on the whole, I agree that the Reformations did more good than harm. Ironically, they may have been especially good for the Catholic Church, as will be clear in Chapter 8. But, in this year of celebrations, I think it appropriate that there be full consideration of the many myths as well as the particular misfortunes that com-plete the picture. That is the task I have undertaken. If that makes me the 'skunk at the picnic', as one of my colleagues suggested, so be it.

1

The myths of full pews, pious kings and limited monarchies

It is well known that by the time Luther rebelled against the Vatican, Europe's churches were very poorly attended. It has long been believed that one of the most immediate and significant results of the Lutheran Reformation was to fill the pews. Moreover, it wasn't only the common folk whose piety was ignited by the great Lutheran revival campaign, but even some of the crowned heads of northern Europe soon were bowed in prayer as they embraced Protestantism. Moreover, after centuries of tyrannical rule by absolute monarchs, the Reformations ushered in a new era of limited monarchies, putting an end to the 'divine right of kings'.

The people's Reformation

The image of medieval piety, of churches filled with devout peasants, has no historical basis. As Michael Walzer put it, 'Medieval society was largely composed of nonpartici- pants in the churches.'[1] Alexander Murray's assessment of medieval religious life has been confirmed again and again: '[S]ubstantial sections of thirteenth-century society hardly attended church at all.'[2] In addition, the locals often misused the church building. In 1367, John Thoresby, the Archbishop of York, fulminated against holding markets in the churches, especially on Sunday. 'Between 1229 and 1367 there were eleven such episcopal injunctions recorded.

Bishop after bishop thundered in vain . . . against those who "turned the house of prayer into a den of thieves".[3] The same thing occurred frequently all across the Continent, as higher officials complained against using churches, even cathedrals, for storing crops and sheltering livestock, and for indoor market days.[4]

It is generally assumed that it was this vacuum that allowed the German Reformation to so quickly and easily become a mass movement. Of course, most social scientists believe that all successful religious movements are based on the 'people', on those with less than an ample share of life's rewards. As Richard Niebuhr (1894–1962) explained in his famous *The Social Sources of Denominationalism*, a new religious movement is always 'a revolt of the poor'.[5] Protestantism was another of the great heresies that arose in Europe because of 'the desire of the poor to improve the material conditions of their lives', as Norman Cohn (1915–2007) put it.[6] Hence, social scientists have long agreed that Lutheranism quickly spread across Germany because it triggered an outburst of religious enthusiasm among the masses. This was greatly facilitated by the fact that Lutheran services were conducted in German instead of Latin and so, for the first time, the average person could understand what was being said. In addition, from earliest days, the Lutherans devoted immense efforts to the religious education of the young. To this end, in 1529 Luther published his *Shorter Catechism*, which soon went through 100,000 copies. Thus he wrote: 'nowadays a girl or boy of fifteen knows more about Christian doctrine than did all the theologians of the great universities in the old days'.[7] Then, in 1543 Luther claimed: 'I do not leave our churches in poor shape; they flourish in pure and sound teaching, and they grow day by day through many excellent and sincere pastors.'[8]

Nevertheless, it didn't happen! The masses in Germany remained as unchurched as ever.

We can be sure of this because teams of inspectors visited the Lutheran churches in many local communities, beginning in 1525 and extending over the next century. These inspectors submitted a huge number of written reports of what they observed – reports that still exist. These documents have been organized and an extensive number of them published by the distinguished American historian Gerald Strauss (1922–2006), who noted, 'I have selected only such instances as could be multiplied a hundredfold.'[9] Consider these excerpts in the light of the fact that in most places the people *were required by law* to attend church services.

In Saxony: 'You'll find more of them out fishing than at service . . . Those who do come walk out as soon as the pastor begins his sermon.'[10] In Seegrehna: 'A pastor testified that he often quits his church without preaching . . . because not a soul has turned up to hear him.'[11] In Coburg: 'Nothing seemed to avail against widespread absenteeism from divine service . . . Groups of men continued to gather in the churchyard to drink brandy and sing bawdy songs while service was being conducted inside.' In Barum: 'It is the greatest and most widespread complaint of all pastors hereabouts that people do not go to church on Sundays . . . Nothing helps; they will not come . . . so that pastors face near-empty churches.'[12] In Braunschweig-Grubenhagen: 'many churches are empty on Sundays'.[13] In Weilburg: 'Absenteeism from church on Sundays was so widespread that the synod debated whether the city gates should be barred on Sunday mornings to lock everyone inside. Evidence from elsewhere suggests that this expedient would not have helped.'[14]

Nevertheless, it is not clear that having a large turnout at Sunday services would have been desirable. That's because when people did come to church, being compelled to do so, many of them misbehaved!

In Nassau: 'Those who come to service are usually drunk . . . and sleep through the whole sermon, except sometimes they fall off the benches, making a great clatter, or women drop their babies on the floor.'[15] In Leipzig:

> [much] absenteeism from services . . . no one punished for it . . . [those who come] play cards while the pastor preaches, and often mock or mimic him cruelly to his face . . . cursing, blaspheming, hooliganism, and fighting are common . . . they enter church when the service is half over, go at once to sleep, and run out again before the blessing is given . . . nobody joins in singing the hymn; it made my heart ache to hear the pastor and the sexton singing all by themselves.[16]

In Wiesbaden: '[during church] there is such snoring that I could not believe my ears when I heard it. The moment these people sit down, they put their heads on their arms and straight away they go to sleep'.[17] In addition, many bring their dogs inside the church, 'barking and snarling so loudly that no one can hear the preacher'.[18] In Hamburg: '[people make] indecent gestures at members of the congregation who wish to join in singing the hymns, even bringing dogs to church so that due to the loud barking the service is disturbed'.[19]

Given these attitudes and lack of attendance, it is hardly surprising that the German masses (and most Europeans) were ignorant of even basic Christian facts. In Saxony: 'In some villages one could not find a single person who knew the ten Commandments.' In Brandenburg: 'A random group of men was . . . asked how they understood each of the ten Commandments, but we found many who could give no answer at all . . . [N]one of them thought it a sin to get dead drunk and curse using the name of God.' In Notenstein:

parishioners 'including church elders, could remember none of the ten Commandments'. In Salzliebenhalle: no one knows 'who their redeemer and savior is'. In Nuremberg: many 'could not name Good Friday as the day of the year when Jesus died'. The pastor at Graim complained: 'Since they never go to church, most of them cannot even say their prayers.'

'It is unnecessary to add that the visitors found everywhere evidence of prodigious drinking, horrible blasphemy, whoring, witchcraft and soothsaying, and widespread contempt for the clergy.'[20] Similar findings hold that things 'were little better in some Calvinist areas of Germany and in the Dutch Republic . . .'[21]

Things were the same in England. The Uniformity Act passed by Parliament in 1552 stated: 'a great number of people in divers parts of this realm . . . do willfully and damnably before Almighty God abstain and refuse to come to their parish churches . . .'[22] Consequently, the ordinary people knew little or nothing of Christianity. As Nicholas Brownd remarked in 1606, the stories in the Bible are 'as strange to them as any news you can tell them'. And a Church of England bishop lamented that not only did the people know nothing from the Scriptures, but 'they know not that there *are* any Scriptures'.[23] At this same time, it was reported that in Wales 'there were thousands of people who knew nothing of Christ – yea almost that never heard of him'.[24]

And it wasn't only the people who knew little or nothing of Christian teachings; many rank-and-file clergy were equally ignorant. When the Bishop of Gloucester systematically tested Church of England diocesan clergy in 1551, of 311 pastors, 171 could not repeat the Ten Commandments, and 27 did not know the author of the Lord's Prayer.[25] The next year, Church of England Bishop Hooper found 'scores of parish clergy who could not tell who was the author of the Lord's Prayer, or where it was to be found'.[26]

Prior to the Reformations, many churchmen had been fully aware of the ignorance of the people. Most assumed this was due to the fact that church services (with the exception of occasional brief homilies) were in Latin, a language that almost no one in the pews could understand. Thus, it was believed that as the Reformations ushered in preaching in the local vernaculars, widespread public ignorance would end. But it didn't. In part, because so few people came to church. In part, because so many who came paid no attention. And, in part, because the emergence of a much better-trained clergy resulted in preaching that was 'far above the capacity of most of their listeners'.[27] The English philosopher John Locke (1632–1704) noted that a preacher 'may as well talk Arabic to a poor day-labourer as the notions' that the Anglican clergy preferred as the basis for their sermons.[28]

By the same token, Martin Luther's efforts to provide religious education for the German peasants and urban lower classes failed completely because the lessons were conceived by a university professor far more concerned with intricate nuances than with the ABCs of Christian belief – not with simply making people familiar with the Lord's Prayer, for example, but with revealing its subtle implications. The heart of Lutheran religious education was Luther's Catechism, which provides a very lengthy explication of basic Christian doctrines. For example, it devotes many pages of rather convoluted text to interpreting each of the Ten Commandments. The local Lutheran clergy were supposed to preach from the Catechism every Sunday afternoon and hold classes for young people during the week.

In most villages these sessions were not held because no one came. That does not mean the people were irreligious, but that:

what parishioners understood as Christianity was never preached from the pulpit or taught in Sunday school, and what they took from the clergy they took on their own terms . . . Since the clergy were incapable of shaping a more popular version of faith, villagers were left to do so themselves.[29]

Even if they hated going to church and knew very little of Christianity, Europeans in the era of the Reformations were not irreligious. But, as Gerald Strauss put it, they 'practiced their own brand of religion, which was a rich compound of ancient rituals, time-bound customs, a sort of unreconstructable folk Catholicism, and a large portion of magic to help them in their daily lives for survival'.[30] The people's religion did often call upon God, Jesus, Mary and various saints, as well as some pagan gods and goddesses (and as frequently invoked minor spirits such as fairies, elves and demons), but it did so only to invoke their aid, having little interest in such matters as salvation. Instead, the emphasis was on pressing, tangible and mundane matters such as health, fertility, weather, sex and good crops. Consequently, the centrepiece of the people's religion was, as it had always been, magic.

Today, little has changed in European religious life. State churches still dominate all of Europe's 'Protestant' nations, with the negative consequences that will be seen in the next chapter. Church attendance remains low everywhere. And magic is still widely embraced!

In 2008 the International Social Survey Project asked people in a number of European nations whether they agreed or disagreed with these three statements:

Some fortune tellers really can foresee the future (fortune tellers).

A person's star sign at birth can affect the course of his or her future (astrology).

Good luck charms do bring good luck (lucky charms).

Table 1.1 shows levels of belief in three nations where a Reformation succeeded and four that remained Catholic. Belief in magic is about equally high on both sides of the denominational divide and rather higher than most would expect in our 'modern' world – and especially in 'secularized' Europe.

Table 1.1   Magical beliefs in Europe in 2008

Nation	Percentage who believe in:		
	Fortune tellers	Astrology	Lucky charms
'Protestant' Nations			
Germany	25	32	37
Netherlands	26	21	19
Switzerland	35	42	36
Catholic Nations			
Austria	28	32	33
France	37	38	23
Ireland	31	17	24
Portugal	27	29	45

Source: International Social Survey Project, 2008.

Pious kings

In many instances, the decision as to whether a particular place would turn Protestant or remain Catholic was 'bound up with the convictions of the head of state'.[31] Throughout the historical literature there are frequent references to the 'piety' of those rulers who chose Protestantism.[32] The 'firm commitment to Lutheranism'[33] of Christian III of Denmark is unquestioned, and the piety of rulers who chose to remain Catholic is often noted, especially in Catholic sources.

Indeed, the point would seem self-evident since these were *religious* choices. Nevertheless, it wasn't so. Everyone knows that Henry VIII was an opportunist. So were most of the others. They became Protestants or remained Catholics, not primarily for religious motives, but depending on how much they stood to gain![34]

Staying Catholic

In 1296 King Philip of France, desperate for funds to continue the war with England, imposed a tax on Church income. Outraged, Pope Boniface VIII issued a bull forbidding taxation of the clergy or of Church property. In response, Philip outlawed the export of money or precious metals and prohibited papal tax collectors from entering France. Subsequently, the papacy moved to Avignon in 1305, partly to be within legal reach of French funds, and remained there until 1378, during which all popes were French. However, even after the papacy moved back to Rome, the Church in France remained subordinate to the Crown. Throughout the fifteenth century the king's authority over the Church expanded. At the start of the sixteenth century this eventuated in substantial reforms of the Church in France (particularly of the monasteries), directed by Cardinal d'Amboise, and empowered by the king. Then, in 1516 the power of the Crown was formalized in the Concordat of Bologna signed by Pope Leo X and King Francis I. The king was acknowledged to have the right to appoint all of the higher posts in the Church of France: the 10 archbishops, 82 bishops, and the priors, abbots and abbesses of all the many hundreds of monasteries, abbeys and convents. Through these appointments, the king gained control of Church property and income. As the distinguished Owen Chadwick (1916–2015) put it,

'When he wanted ecclesiastical money, his methods need not even be devious.'[35] This removed a very considerable temptation for the French regime to support Protestantism.

'In Spain, as in France, no Reformation was needed to subordinate the Church to the State.'[36] The Spanish Crown had long held the right to nominate archbishops and bishops, to fine the clergy, and to receive a substantial share of the tithe. Spanish control of the Church greatly increased in 1486 when Ferdinand and Isabella gained the right to make all major ecclesiastical appointments, to prohibit appeals from Spanish courts to Rome, and to impose taxes on the clergy.[37] Indeed, it was illegal to publish papal bulls and decrees in Spain or its possessions without prior royal consent – which is why, decades later, the pope's decrees against slavery could not be read in Spain's slave-holding colonies in the New World.[38] These same conditions prevailed in Portugal.

The subordination of the Church to the state increased under Charles V (1500–58), as Spain became the centre of the Holy Roman Empire, extending its power to the Netherlands, Austria, portions of south-eastern 'Germany', and most of the Italian city states. Although Charles incurred huge costs in defending and attempting to extend his vast holdings, the lure of Church property was more than offset by three factors. First, he already was receiving a substantial portion of Church income. Second, the pope's support was valuable in helping Charles sustain his claims to sovereignty, especially in Spain where he was always regarded as an 'outsider'. Third, the immense flow of gold and silver from the New World reduced the relative value of Church wealth to such an extent that it seemed not worth the risks involved in confiscating it.

In early days, Protestantism proved to be popular in Poland and was tolerated by the state, which had long respected the religious rights of Jews and Eastern Orthodox Christians. Eventually, however, Polish Protestantism was suppressed, and a large contingent of Jesuits was brought in to assist in reinstituting Roman Catholic hegemony. Why? Because the ambitions of the restive lower nobility and of the burghers, as well as the factionalism within Protestantism, seemed to threaten the Crown, and because the Church had already surrendered much of its wealth and power to the Polish nobility. Church lands and the clergy were taxed. Only members of Polish noble families could hold higher Church offices, and local lords controlled the appointment of parish clergy. Thus, no windfall profits tempted the Polish Crown to embrace Protestantism. As Robert Wuthnow put it, the Polish nobility 'enjoyed sufficient control over the church that they had little incentive to turn toward Protestantism'.[39]

Becoming 'Protestants'

In contrast, in other parts of Europe the enormous value of Church property, and the Church's continuing financial extractions, served as powerful temptations and bitter grievances. So long as there had been only One Church, it was risky to challenge papal authority, as Henry IV discovered when he was kept waiting barefoot in the snow by Pope Gregory VII. But now, Lutheranism offered an alternative source of religious legitimacy, making excommunication an empty threat. This was why so many German princes rallied to Luther: they gained huge amounts of immediate wealth by seizing Church property (in some places the Church owned half of the land), and they continued to benefit from the flow of tithes and legacies to the state churches which they controlled. Of course, this did not apply to the German prince-bishops, since they already owned the Church property and netted most of the Church income (although they did have to send money to Rome), and not one of them opted to become Lutheran.

As for the English Reformation, Henry VIII was never a Protestant. He was quite opposed to central Protestant doctrines and continued to burn some Lutherans and Lollards! So Henry could not even pretend to be motivated by theology. He merely declared an English, rather than a Roman, Catholic Church, with himself as head, rather than the pope. That act alone would have sufficed to enable him to take and shed wives as he saw fit. Of course, he could not leave in place those church officials and members of religious orders who disputed him as the head of the Church, but having made what replacements were necessary there was no need to dissolve all the monasteries and convents. But he did, thereby gaining enormous wealth. Consider that from the shrine dedicated to St Thomas à Becket alone, Henry's agents confiscated 4,994 ounces of gold, 4,425 ounces of silver gilt, 5,286 ounces of silver and 26 cartloads of other treasure – and this was regarded at the time as but a trivial portion of the wealth confiscated from the Church.[40] And trivial it was, given that it is estimated that Henry gained about £87 billion (in today's money)[41] per year from his initial seizures and millions more subsequently.[42]

In Denmark, at the dawn of the sixteenth century from a third to half of all the tillable land was owned by the Church, and everyone else paid tithes – substantial amounts of which went to Rome. The pope also made all ecclesiastical appointments. In 1534 Christian III became king. As a boy of 18, Christian had met Luther at the Diet of Worms and was very impressed. This fact alone has led numerous authors to credit his making Denmark a Protestant state entirely out of religious concerns. Perhaps. But it also must be noted that Christian was very impressed with the confiscations of Church property and wealth by the Protestant princes in Germany. Once upon the throne, he declared Denmark a Protestant state and immediately seized all Church property and redirected the tithes to the royal treasury. What were his motives? Of course, he said they were religious. And perhaps they were. But he could have left the Church property in the hands of the new Lutheran Church. But he didn't.

Meanwhile, Sweden successfully rebelled against Denmark's rule as Gustavus Vasa drove the Danes out of Sweden and was formally crowned King Gustavus I in 1528. Here, too, the Church had enjoyed unchallenged authority and enormous wealth. When the new king deposed an uncooperative archbishop and nominated replacements for four empty bishoprics, the pope supported the deposed archbishop and rejected Gustavus's nominees. To this affront was added the fact that the new king was in desperate need of funds. He dealt with both concerns by declaring Sweden to be a Protestant state, and by appropriating 'the possessions and revenues of the Church'.[43] To strengthen his support among the nobility, Gustavus sold them expropriated Church land at rock bottom bargain prices. Even so, the Church property Gustavus kept increased the Crown lands fourfold.[44]

In addition, in many circumstances it was in the self-interest even of ordinary citizens that Church property be confiscated and Church authority curtailed. For example, the 65 Free Imperial Cities (so-called because they were free from control by local nobility and answered only, and barely, to the Holy Roman Emperor) were severely burdened with extensive, untaxed Church properties, and with large numbers of resident clergy and members of religious orders who refused to perform the duties required of other citizens. In most of these cities at least one-third of the property belonged to the Church and as many as a tenth of the residents were clergy and members of orders.[45] In nearly every city there was substantial conflict between Church and city over special privileges, mainly because of the magnitude of the Church's presence.[46] The clergy exempted themselves from all taxes. This was a daily grievance because in most cities there was a sales tax on consumer items, such as wine and beer, which was not paid by the local priests, monks and nuns. Everyone else paid property taxes, but not the Church – indeed everyone else was required to pay tithes to the Church. In similar fashion, when a citizen was accused of a crime, he or she stood trial before a local court and was at great risk of the death penalty – in those days people were routinely executed for quite minor crimes. No matter their offence, priests, monks and nuns could be tried only by a religious court and ran nearly no risk of the death penalty or even a very severe sentence – murderers were often sentenced to several years of fasting. Nor would the clergy or members of orders fulfil such duties as taking their turn standing guard at night on the city walls, as all other able-bodied men were required to do. Hence, all lay people in these cities had a stake in shifting to Protestantism and about two-thirds of these cities did so.[47]

To sum up: self-interest played a very major role in deciding who opted to turn Protestant or to remain Catholic.

Limited monarchies

It is commonly claimed that the Reformations put an end to the doctrine of the 'divine right of kings', thereby revealing the entirely worldly basis of royal authority. Prior to that time, 'belief in the God-given authority of monarchs was central to the Roman Catholic vision of governance in the Middle Ages'.[48] Jared Rubin claimed that, lacking the support of the Church elite, Protestant monarchs had to turn to parliaments for support and thereby shared their power.[49] Thus, the Reformations inaugurated a new age of limited monarchies.

This is nonsense. The Church never endorsed the notion of the divine right of kings. That was first proclaimed by James I of England (1566–1625), a Protestant after whom the King James Version of the Bible is named. Instead, the Catholic Church always asserted that its authority was greater than that of monarchs. From St Augustine through St Thomas Aquinas, the great Church theologians denied the moral authority of the state and condemned tyrants, warranting their overthrow. Moreover, the Church was entirely at ease with the limited democracies that evolved in the Italian city states long before any Reformations and in 1215 the English bishops participated in forcing King John to sign the Magna Carta. Finally, by taking control of the Church as well as the state, many 'Protestant' monarchs were far more powerful than had been the case in these same kingdoms prior to the Reformations. Indeed, Luther fully supported 'the development of strong centralized states and absolute monarchies'.[50]

Now for the details.

In his great work *The City of God*, written in about 410, Augustine revealed that although the state was essential for an orderly society, it still was lacking in fundamental legitimacy:

> What are kingdoms but great robberies? For what are robberies themselves, but little kingdoms? The band itself is made up of men; it is ruled by the authority of a prince, it is knit together by the pact of confederacy; the booty is divided by the law agreed on. If, by the admittance of abandoned men, this evil increases to such a degree that it holds places, fixes abodes, takes possession of cities, and subdues peoples,

> it assumes more plainly the name of kingdom, because reality is now manifestly conferred on it, not by the removal of covetousness, but by the addition of impunity. Indeed, that was the apt and true reply which was given to Alexander the Great by a pirate who had been seized. For when the king had asked the man what he meant by keeping hostile possession of the sea, he answered with bold pride, 'What thou meanest by seizing the whole earth; but because I do it in a petty ship, I am called a robber, whilst thou who doest it with a great fleet art styled emperor.'[51]

This 'shocking realism'[52] has often surprised and upset Augustine's readers. But, given the immense authority of the writer, this view shaped Christian political sensibilities ever after: Christian writers could not condemn suggestions for liberalizing the state, or even for dispensing with monarchies. Moreover, by affirming the secularity of kingship the Church made it possible to examine the basis for worldly power and the interplay of rights and rule. Late in the fourteenth century John Wycliffe pointed out that if kings were chosen by God and ruled with divine rights, then God must assist and approve the sins of tyrants – 'a blasphemous conclusion'.[53] Hence it was not a sin to depose tyrants.

That had already been acknowledged a century earlier by Thomas Aquinas, if a bit grudgingly. Having warned of the many perils of acting to remove a tyrant, including the fact that all too often an even worse tyranny results, Aquinas wrote in *On Kingship*: 'If to provide itself with a king belongs to the right of a given multitude, it is not unjust that the king be deposed or have his power restricted by that same multitude if, becoming a tyrant, he abuses his royal power.' However, Aquinas counselled that a 'scheme should be carefully worked out which would prevent the multitude ruled by a king from falling into the hands of a tyrant'.[54] And, in various forms, that is precisely what went on in many European domains, with the full support of the Church.

In England in 1215, a coalition of nobles and Church officials, including all of the bishops as well as the master of the Knights Templar, imposed the Magna Carta on King John, severely limiting royal power. At about the same time, republican forms of government evolved in several of the Italian city states, including Venice, Genoa, Florence and Milan. Each of them came to be ruled by elected assemblies based on extensive suffrage, including members of the various workers' guilds. In every case the Church played a vigorous role in supporting and even in advocating these changes – indeed the Church often ventured into the political arena on behalf of expanding the voting franchise.

Of course, most of Europe continued to be ruled by kings and princes. But these medieval monarchs were limited, in fact as well as in principle, by the role of the clergy who served them both as confessors and as advisers. In the latter role the clergy were powerful because of their ability to provide intelligence and serve as channels of communication. Through the network of clergy serving the entire nobility of Europe, clergy serving in any given court could provide otherwise unavailable information on the character, aims, intentions and resources of potential adversaries – intelligence provided by fellow clergy serving in the same capacity elsewhere. In addition they could and often did serve as intermediaries and typically exerted their influence to prevent warfare. Indeed, a number of popes, including the illustrious Gregory VII (1020–85), devoted immense efforts to imposing a 'truce of God' on the feudal nobility.

In addition, the role of clergy as confessors was often of even greater significance. Given their power to give or to withhold absolution, confessors often imposed moral limits on monarchs who otherwise could have acted with impunity. Indeed, the flow of pilgrims to the Holy Land was swelled by members of the nobility, acting on the demand of their confessors that they do this in order to obtain absolution for their serious misdeeds. Even some of the most brutal offenders went, some of them barefoot all the way. Thus, Fulk III, Count of Anjou (972–1040), a hot-headed brute, was required to make four pilgrimages to Jerusalem, dying on the way home from the last. The point being that the Church very significantly limited the power of medieval monarchs. Indeed, Henry VIII could not get a divorce!

Those limits ended when monarchs became the head of state churches. Who now could tell Henry VIII he could not divorce? Who now could tell any German prince who headed his own Lutheran Church that he stood in mortal peril for his soul? In fact, Martin Luther stressed that very fact, claiming 'that secular government is an ordinance ordained by God and that the special rule claimed by the Roman Pontiff over things secular was an usurpation of the power committed by God to the secular authority'.[55] Moreover, 'Luther's political thought began with the assumption that God had given rulers their office and that rebellion against those divinely appointed rulers was tantamount to rebellion against God'.[56] No pope would have agreed.

Control of their state churches greatly increased the power of monarchs. Not only did it give them free access to churchly wealth, but they also could and did use the powers of the state on behalf of their churches. In Chapter 2 we will examine laws requiring acts of piety, including mandatory church attendance. The monarchs also exploited their position as head of the Church to inflate their legitimacy with claims of being semi-divine. In 1665, the Kingdom of Denmark-Norway adopted a written constitution for the first time. In it was this:

[the Monarch] shall from this day forth be revered and considered the most perfect and supreme person on earth by all his subjects, standing above all human laws and having no judge above his person, neither in spiritual nor temporal matters, except God alone.[57]

This authorized the king to do away with all other centres of power, including the abolition of the Council of the Realm, a sort of parliamentary body. How's that for a 'limited' monarchy?

Twelve years earlier, the Diet of Brandenburg met for the last time and gave Frederick William, the Great Elector, power to raise taxes without its consent. Later in the century, King Charles XI of Sweden achieved 'absolute rule'. After the death of his son in 1718, parliamentary rule was instituted, but King Gustavus III seized all power back in 1771.

To sum up: three great myths about the consequences of the Reformations have been exposed. The Reformations did not fill the pews or convert the masses to a coherent Christianity. The people continued to stay away from church in droves and held on to their mixture of Christian and pagan religious notions. Monarchs did not embrace a Reformation or remain steadfastly Catholic primarily for religious reasons, but out of self-interest. Henry VIII not only got his divorce; he also gained incredible wealth by looting the monasteries. The same was true all across northern Europe, as kings and princes declared for Lutheranism and seized the wealth of the Church. In contrast, the King of France and the Holy Roman Emperor already had substantial control of the Church and shared in its wealth. Finally, the Reformations substantially increased the absolute power of monarchs by dispensing with their need to answer to the Church either as rulers or personally.

2

The misfortune of state churches, forced piety and bigotry

One might well suppose that, given their personal trials, leaders of the Reformations (aside from Henry VIII) would have agreed that the religious life requires freedom of thought – that religion is a matter of conscience and therefore requires policies of toleration. Certainly that is strongly implied in Martin Luther's famous conclusion of his testimony before the Diet of Worms: 'I cannot and will not recant anything, for to go against conscience is neither right nor safe. Here I stand, I can do no other. So help me God. Amen.'

And early on Luther did support religious freedom, writing that the secular government must 'allow people to believe what they . . . want, and they must use no coercion in this matter against anyone'.[1] Unfortunately, Luther only felt this way while he was an excommunicated underdog. Once the Lutheran churches were secure, Luther, like most other leaders of the Reformations, believed in freedom of conscience only for those who agreed with him.[2] Brutal, repressive bigotry was a hallmark of the various Reformations, and the relative silence on these matters by generations of historians is shameful. Of course, there has been full coverage of the many religious wars stemming from the Reformations, and of the savagery these involved – but these were wars, not matters of domestic policy. In contrast, it is extremely difficult to find any published literature on the remarkably repressive character of the Lutheran state churches in northern Europe. Many books and essays on the history of the Scandinavian Lutheran churches, for example, hail the beginning of an era of limited 'religious liberty' in the nineteenth century, but offer no details about the utter lack of religious liberty in prior centuries; they don't even mention that everyone was forced by law to attend church and take Communion.[3] Eventually, by consulting more than 20 books and finding an occasional sentence here and there, I pieced together enough material to write the section. It was nearly as difficult to discover some of the similarly repressive efforts of the Church of England, as will be noted. But even more shocking is how little has been published, even in German, about the linkage between Reformation-based anti-Semitism and the subsequent catastrophes culminating in the Holocaust. Worse yet, much that has been written attempts to wish it all away.

In this chapter I shall try to fill these gaps, if only briefly.

Repressive state churches

All three Reformations gave rise to state churches – monopoly institutions ruled by heads of state and sustained by laws that were enforced by civil authorities. In contrast, being unwilling to subordinate itself to control by the state, the Roman Catholic Church was never in a position to attempt to legally force individual acts of piety and, perhaps, too sophisticated to attempt it. But that is precisely what the Reformation-based state churches tried to do. The masses were going to be devout, whether they liked it or not!

Lutheran state churches

From the start, the German princes who supported Luther were not going to allow themselves to be exploited or commanded by religious leaders again. Henceforth, they would rule both Church and state. In this they were vigorously supported by Martin Luther, whose 'advice to the German princes who embraced Protestantism was that they compel their subjects to submit to religious instruction and allow them to hear only authorized preachers'.[4] In 1541, Luther wrote that he 'could not conceive of any reason by which [religious] toleration could be justified before God'.[5] Indeed, not only Luther, but Calvin and his associates such as Martin Bucer, and probably even Henry VIII, 'could not conceive of a divided church'.[6]

Thus, the creation of Lutheran state churches brought no religious freedom, but merely replaced the monopoly Roman Catholic churches with a new brand of monopoly churches. Moreover, being in a position not merely to rule their churches, but to impose laws, the German princes soon began attempts to dictate individual religiousness. Laws requiring a certain frequency of church attendance, the taking of Communion, and baptism of infants soon appeared all across the Lutheran areas of Germany. So did laws excluding all religious nonconformists, especially Jews. Indeed, Landgrave Philip of Hesse even required that the Jews in his domain attend Christian church services.[7]

Efforts to force personal piety soon spread to Scandinavia. Several years after Gustavus I had created the Church of Sweden, it became the law that every resident must belong to the state Lutheran Church:

> The punishment for those who apostasized from the Lutheran faith . . . was exile and loss of the right to inheritance . . . The only group who were generally exempt from this law were foreign ambassadors . . . in 1624, two Swedish converts to Catholicism were put to death in Stockholm.[8]

But belonging to the Evangelical Lutheran Church was not enough. Everyone was required by law to attend church regularly. Allowances were made for those living in remote areas, especially in the north and during the winter, to attend less often. Subsequently, King Charles XI (1655–97) 'put soldiers on the street on Sunday, in time of divine service, to ensure that everyone was in church'.[9] In addition, the Canon Law of 1686 ordered all Swedes to receive Communion three times a year;[10] those who failed to do so could not be married or buried and they were denied a 'migration certificate'[11] – an internal passport that was needed in order to move one's residence or even to travel within Sweden. In 1726, Sweden adopted the Conventicle Act which prohibited more than three people gathering for prayer or Bible study without a member of the Lutheran clergy being present – the point being to prevent any groups of religious dissenters from forming.[12]

In Norway and Denmark (which were a single kingdom in those days), things were much the same. It was impossible to be a citizen without being a Lutheran. In 1735 the king imposed a sabbatarian law. 'No amusements on Sundays were allowed and people who did not go to church were fined. Shortly after the Royal Theatre closed.'[13] In 1736 it became compulsory for every citizen to be baptized, to be confirmed, to be wed and to be buried by church ceremonies. In 1741 Denmark joined Sweden in adopting a Conventical Act.[14]

Calvinist state churches

The attempts to use the law to force piety by the Lutheran state churches seem puny when compared with Calvin's Geneva.[15]

Attendance at Sunday morning services was mandatory. In addition, if there were sermons preached during the week (and usually there were several), attendance at these also was required by law. Being late to church was subject to a fine.

To speak disrespectfully of Calvin or the clergy was a crime that could lead to imprisonment or banishing.

The colour and quantity of clothing were limited by law. There was a legal limit on the number of dishes it was permissible to serve at a meal. Gambling, card-playing, frequenting taverns (although there were none), singing indecent or irreligious songs were all prohibited.

'Immodesty' in dress was outlawed. A woman was jailed for arranging her hair at an 'immoral height'.

Children could only be named after characters in the Old Testament.

Fornication was punished by exile or by drowning – there were instances of each. Adultery carried a mandatory death penalty and Calvin's own stepdaughter and son-in-law were executed on this charge.

Blasphemy and idolatry were punished by death.

In one case a child was executed for striking his parents.

Despite this ferocious approach to enforced piety, it seems to have had only limited success, as the continuing need to impose punishments attests.

In remarkable contrast, the Calvinists in the Dutch Republic opted for official policies of religious freedom and toleration – perhaps influenced by the commercial advantages of trading across Europe's denominational lines. Lutherans and Anabaptists were welcome and so were Jews.

The Church of England

In 1536 the first Act of Supremacy made Henry VIII, and subsequent monarchs, supreme head of the Church of England. As had taken place throughout the Lutheran north, the creation of a state church soon led to the royal seizure of huge amounts of Catholic Church wealth and lands, especially with the Dissolution of the Monasteries. And as head of the Church, Henry VIII executed some Catholics, Lutherans, Anabaptists and various other religious dissenters. However, Henry made no effort to legislate personal piety. But his daughter did.

On 8 May 1559 Elizabeth I gave her approval to the Act of Uniformity which had been passed by Parliament on 29 April. The primary purpose of the Act was to make the *Book of Common Prayer and Administration of Sacraments* mandatory for use by all English clerics. Moreover, the Act included a clause specifying fines and imprisonment for all who in any way denigrated or even criticized the book. In addition, well down in the text, and almost incidentally, the Act required everyone to attend church regularly:

> all and every person and persons inhabiting within this realm, or any other [of] the majesty's dominions, shall diligently and faithfully, having no lawful or reasonable excuse to be absent, endeavour themselves to resort to their parish church or chapel . . . upon every Sunday and other days ordained and used to be kept as holy days, and then and there to abide orderly and . . . soberly during the time of common prayers, preachings, or other service of God . . . upon pain that every person so offending shall forfeit for every such offence twelve pence[16] . . . [Twelve pence in 1559 amounted to about two weeks' wages for a skilled workman.]

This law was doubly repressive since it was meant not only to improve the very low rates of attendance (see Chapter 1), but to expose Catholic recusants, since they could be expected to avoid non-Catholic services.

It probably is not surprising that this legal undertaking by the Church of England is ignored in the major historical works on the Reformations. After all, they also ignore the far more extensive attempts to coerce piety in the Lutheran nations. But it seems odd that this effort is also given short shrift in recent works on the history of the Church of England – Hervé Picton's excellent 2015 volume deals with several aspects of Elizabeth's impact on the Church, but not this. Fortunately, I was able to discover a fine recent scholarly paper on the topic by Clive D. Field.[17] And Field's paper reveals what may be the primary reason scholars have chosen to ignore the legal effort to force the English to attend church. It was a dismal failure.

Non-compliance with the law was so massive and widespread that very little effort was made to enforce it. One leading pastor complained that 'not one in twenty in many towns go to any place of worship on the Lord's Day'.[18] Those few who were charged under the law usually pleaded that they were being unfairly charged since most others in the area were equally guilty. Thus, William Sorrell of Great Bardfield complained in 1599 that at the time he was accused, 'there was not above 20 or 40 people at church' out of more than 200 in the parish.[19]

Finally, on 4 April 1687, James II issued a Declaration of Indulgence:

All and all manner of penal laws in matters ecclesiastical, for not coming to church or not receiving the sacrament or for any other nonconformity to the religion established or for or by reason of exercise of religion in any other manner whatsoever, be immediately suspended.[20]

From then on it was legal to spend one's Sundays 'betweixt the bedd and the chimney corner and sauntering about the streets and fields (not to speake of eating and drinkeing)'.[21]

However, there was to be no 'indulgence' of Catholicism. Between 1559 and 1610, 'Parliament passed a series of harsh penal codes . . . that made it unlawful, and indeed treason-able, to engage in Catholic rites. Catholics could not hear a Mass, join a profession, hold office, own a weapon or come within 10 miles of London. Priests were banned from the country, and anyone harboring them could be condemned to death.'[22]

The modern legacy

That the Reformations resulted in repressive state churches is not merely a misfortune of historical interest. The defects of state churches continue to be responsible for many of the current weaknesses of religion in Europe. In contrast with places such as the United States and sub-Saharan Africa, where extensive pluralism has created a marketplace filled with very aggressively competitive religious 'firms' with the result of high rates of attendance, the state churches in Europe have been lazy and ineffective, while their basic character, including even their doctrines, often has been subject to gross interference by the state.

All of this was anticipated long ago by Adam Smith, who pointed out that the clergy in state churches are inevitably content to repose 'themselves upon their benefices [while neglecting] to keep up the devotion of the great body of the people; and having given themselves up to indolence . . . become altogether incapable of making any vigorous exer-tion . . .'[23] Hence, from early days 'absenteeism was rife'[24] among the Lutheran clergy as well as those of the Church of England. This was particularly true of clergy assigned to rural villages who tended to close their churches for the winter and reside in the nearest city. In addition, being state churches, they are ruled by state authorities even when it comes to matters of doctrine. Here it will be useful to focus on the Scandinavian state churches.

There are Lutheran state churches in Denmark, Finland, Iceland and Norway, and although the Church of Sweden lost its established position in 2006, the government continues to collect a religious tax on its behalf. The clergy of these state churches (including the Swedish Church) are civil servants, belong to trade unions, and have the right to strike. They are nearly impossible to fire. A priest in the Danish Church attracted international attention when he published a book proclaiming his atheism. He was quoted in a national newspaper thus: 'God belongs in the past. He actually is so old fashioned that I am baffled by modern people believing in his existence. I am thoroughly fed up with empty words about miracles and eternal life.'[25] After a hearing, he was returned to his parish pulpit.

As clerical civil servants, the Lutheran clergy are not concerned about lack of attendance (it runs at 2 to 3 per cent a week), because their salaries do not depend upon the offering plate. Nor have they made any significant protests when the state has taken it upon itself to impose new doctrines. For many years, Sweden's Minister of Ecclesiastical Affairs was Alva Myrdal, wife of the famous economist Gunnar Myrdal, and herself a famous leftist economist and nonbeliever. In 1972 she appointed a government commission to compose a new translation of the New Testament for 'general cultural reasons'. It was published in 1981, and even the most ardent supporters acknowledge that it contains 'sweeping transformation[s] of accepted interpretations . . . In important ways, it must of necessity run against the grain of Bible traditions.'[26] Among other 'corrections', the new version omits the miracles. It was made the official Church of Sweden version by government fiat. Similarly, in Denmark, Parliament authorized female pastors in the state church without referring the matter to church bishops.[27] Indeed, throughout Scandinavia government officials assert their full authority over the churches – which stand nearly empty everywhere.

The Church of England has, in recent times, been far less subject to state interference, although all measures adopted by the General Synod of the Church must be approved by both Houses of Parliament. However, as in Scandinavia, the Church of England clergy are unionized and recently forced the Church to rescind a rule defrocking clergy convicted of felonies, on grounds that such convictions might have been miscarriages of justice. Also like the Lutheran state churches, the Church of England faces low and declining rates of attendance. However, Sarah Mullally, the fourth woman to be appointed a bishop, reassured her colleagues that this should not be taken too seriously as the people will 'still encounter God', even if only through sources such as Facebook.[28]

In any event, a recent study by two economists, based on surveys from 59 nations, found that the presence of state churches very substantially reduced rates of church attendance.[29]

Hatred and intolerance

Christianity was born in hatred and intolerance. Romans made a sport of killing Christians in strange ways, and converts to the early Church had to survive two great and bloody persecution campaigns before the Emperor Constantine made them secure. According to Roman officials the Christians' crime was 'atheism' – like the Jews, they denied the divinity of Rome's many gods. It is fundamental to all monotheisms that the commitment to One God requires denial of all other godly claims. In the first known instance of monotheism, Pharaoh Amenhotep IV closed all of the temples to Egypt's many gods, requiring the sole worship of Aten.

In addition, it usually has been concluded that if there is only One God there can be only One Church. Consequently, once fully in power, the Christian Church headed by the pope in Rome tolerated no competition. This resulted in a series of bloody repressions as 'heretical' movements erupted again and again. In fact, the crucial difference between Lutheranism and groups such as the Waldensians and the Cathars was the military might of the German princes.

Consequently, the Reformations bear no burden for having initiated religious hatred and intolerance among Christians, but the 'Protestants' also learned nothing about tolerance from their own persecution. What they did was to raise the level and duration of conflict precisely because they were sustained by armed force – Europe's religious wars raged for centuries. In addition, these conflicts generated vicious forms of prejudice and discrimination, by both sides, that lasted well into modern times.[30]

In addition, there is the matter of anti-Semitism.

Reformations and the Jews

The situation of Jews in Europe prior to the Reformations differed from place to place, but they always lived under the stigma of rejecting Jesus. Nevertheless, the more odious restrictions – such as being confined at night to ghettos, or even being expelled from a nation – were placed upon them by the state, not the Roman Catholic Church. Indeed, the Church was a reliable barrier against anti-Jewish violence, as I reported at length in a previous book.[31] Forced conversions were condemned and the Church frequently took action to prevent and to punish attacks on Jews – clergy often risked their own lives to protect local Jews when anti-Semitic attacks broke out. This is attested again and again by medieval Jewish sources and by modern-day

Jewish historians. As the distinguished Robert Chazan noted, despite being the objects of suspicion and enduring many forms of discrimination, 'the essential fact remained [that it was official Church policy] that Jews were to be permitted to exist within Christian society and to fulfill their religious obligations as Jews'.[32]

The English Reformation had no consequences for the Jews because they had all been expelled from the country by Edward I in 1290, and only readmitted by Oliver Cromwell in 1655, although their residence in England wasn't legalized until 1829! In 1846 the law imposing a special dress code upon Jews was repealed. And in 1858, Jews were allowed to be Members of Parliament – more than a decade before Catholics were allowed to enrol in Oxford and Cambridge.

John Calvin was anti-Semitic as were other Calvinist leaders, but he could do nothing but talk because the Jews had been expelled from Geneva in 1491. Moreover, Calvin's antagonism towards the Jews was trivial in contrast with the virulent anti-Semitism of Martin Luther.

Luther's anti-Semitism and its consequences

In 2012, in his fine book *Martin Luther's Anti-Semitism*, the distinguished American scholar and Lutheran seminary professor Eric W. Gritsch (1931–2012) regretted that the

International Congress of Luther Research, meeting every four or five years since 1956, has dealt with almost every topic in lectures and seminars except with the issue of 'Luther and the Jews.'[33]

Gritsch also found it 'astonishing that the icon of German historiography, Leopold von Ranke, wrote the classic work *German History in the Age of Reformation* without saying anything about Luther's attitude to the Jews when [Ranke was] dealing with their persecution'!

Unlike some recent Lutheran writers who have attempted to soft-pedal Luther's anti-Semitism, or at least to argue that it had no impact on the Nazis or for their support,[34] Gritsch wrote a book that not only carefully confronted Luther's venomous attacks on the Jews, but assessed how Luther's writing had been utilized by the Nazis.

Prior to this, Gritsch had published nine books, including *The Wit of Martin Luther*. All nine were published by Fortress Press, the official publishing house of the Evangelical Lutheran Church in America. But Fortress did not publish Gritsch's last volume. Instead, it was brought out by Eerdmans, a house long informally associated with the Dutch Reformed Church. That seems consistent with the lukewarm and hair-splitting reviews given the book by Lutheran writers – the book was mostly ignored in other quarters.

The response to Gritsch by Lutheran reviewers was fully in keeping with my encounter with Lutheran theologians when, at the start of my career, I did a major study of the effects of Christian faith on anti-Semitism, based on opinion surveys of Americans.[35] As I worked on the project, I happened to read William Shirer's *The Rise and Fall of the Third Reich*, and became aware, for the first time, of Martin Luther's anti-Semitism, when I read:

> It is difficult to understand the behavior of most German Protestants in the first Nazi years unless one is aware of two things: their history and the influence of Martin Luther. The great founder of Protestantism was both a passionate anti-Semite and a ferocious believer in absolute obedience to political authority. He wanted Germany rid of the Jews. Luther's advice was literally followed four centuries later by Hitler, Goering, and Himmler.[36]

Since, in connection with my anti-Semitism project, I had access to several prominent Lutheran theologians, I brought this to their attention. Each of them quickly reassured me that it was well known that Shirer had exaggerated; that Luther's anti-Semitism was long forgotten and played no role in influencing modern opinions. I believed them. But they were at least wrong. Luther's anti-Semitism had a dreadful impact on European Jewry, both immediately and centuries later in Nazi Germany.

On the Jews and Their Lies by Martin Luther

In his early days as a leader of the German Reformation, Luther expressed great sympathy for the Jews and assumed that they would soon convert to his brand of Christianity, since it now was cleansed of its papal distortions. In an essay: 'That Jesus Christ Was Born a Jew', written in 1523, Luther noted:

> When we are inclined to boast of our position we should remember that we are but Gentiles, while the Jews are of the image of Christ. We are aliens and in-laws; they are blood relatives, cousins, and brothers of the Lord . . .
>
> If we really want to help them, we must be guided in our dealings with them by the law of Christian love. We must receive them cordially . . . If some of them should prove stiff-necked, what of it? After all, we ourselves are not all good Christians either.

By 1538, Luther had realized that the Jews were not going to convert. Thus, he wrote that 'it is evident that he [God] has forsaken them, that they can no longer be his people . . .' Then, having brooded on the matter for another five years, Luther wrote a 'little book so that I may be found among them who opposed such poisonous activities of the Jews and who warned Christians to be on their guard against them'. Thus did he introduce *On the Jews and Their Lies*.[37] It is as violently inflammatory as any anti-Semitic tract ever written.

The heart of the matter lies in Luther's rhetorical question: 'What shall we Christians do with this rejected and condemned people, the Jews?' Luther offered seven actions.

First, to set fire to their synagogues and schools . . .

Second, I advise that their houses also be razed and destroyed.

Third, I advise that all their prayer books and Talmudic writings, in which such idolatry, lies, cursing and blasphemy are taught, be taken from them.

Fourth, I advise that their rabbis be forbidden to teach henceforth on pain of loss of life and limb . . .

Fifth, I advise that safe-conduct on the highways be abolished completely for Jews. For they have no business in the countryside . . .

Sixth, I advise that usury be prohibited to them, and that all cash and treasure of silver and gold be taken from them . . .

Seventh, I recommend putting a flail, an axe, a hoe, a spade, a distaff, or a spindle into the hands of young, strong Jews and Jewesses and letting them earn their bread in the sweat of their brow . . . But if we are afraid that they might harm us . . . then let us emulate the common sense of other nations . . . [and] eject them forever from the country.

Should you be tempted to sigh with relief that at least Luther stopped short of proposing a 'final solution', Luther noted that '[w]e are not at fault in slaying them'.

Consequences

As I did the research needed to write this chapter I was stunned not only by the extent of the silence on the Nazi use of Luther's attacks on the Jews, but even more by the predominance of apologists among those who did acknowledge it. Again and again, I read that the Nazis were racial anti-Semites while Luther was 'merely' a religious anti-Semite.[38] James Kittleson (1941–2003) claimed that 'Luther never became an anti-Semite in the modern, racial sense of the term'.[39] The point being that Luther was willing to absolve and accept Jewish converts to Christianity, so his proposed pogroms applied only to Jews who remained Jewish. The Nazis cared only about 'race', about a person's heritage, and rejected the value or validity of conversion. In the Nazi view, your parents may have been good Lutherans, but if your grandparents were Jews, you were racially a Jew and subject to their racial policies, whereas Luther would have exempted you. Granted there is something here. But it seems very little given what Luther proposed to do about Jews who did not convert (and his belief that few if any could be converted). Nor did it inhibit the extensive campaign by the Nazis to show that Luther was on their side.

A second line of defence of Luther has been to argue that there was not an 'unbroken link' of intellectual descent from Luther to Hitler; ergo the one did not lead to the other. It is noted that many notorious early nineteenth-century anti-Semites, even those in Germany, did not cite Luther. Uwe Siemon-Netto argued that the Nazis were anti-Semites before they revived Luther's works. But no serious scholar has proposed that Martin Luther caused Hitler or his henchmen to become anti-Semites. What is at issue is whether Luther's anti-Semitism was helpful in increasing the credibility of Nazi claims about the Jews – was Luther's anti-Semitism effectively exploited by the Nazis? And, being superb propagandists, the Nazis made everyone in Germany fully aware that Luther was on their side about the Jews. Perhaps even more important was the fact that leading Lutheran clerics confirmed and ratified the Nazi claims about Luther and about the Jews.

As for the Nazis, 1933 was the 450th anniversary of the birth of Martin Luther, and in addition to the many celebrations held by the Lutheran churches, the Nazi Party held a number of celebrations too. At one of these celebrations, the prominent Nazi Erich Koch made a speech comparing Hitler and Luther, claiming that the Nazis fought with Luther's spirit.[40] Soon after, the Nazis reprinted Luther's 'little book' on the Jews and gave it maximum publicity and circulation. They exhibited Luther's book in a glass case at all of the party's annual rallies in Nuremberg. With a great deal of fanfare and press coverage, the city of Nuremberg presented an original first edition of Luther's *On The Jews and Their Lies* to Julius Streicher, editor of the Nazi newspaper *Der Stürmer*, on his birthday in 1937. Glowing with pride, Streicher said that Luther's work was the most radically anti-Semitic tract ever written. In 1940, Heinrich Himmler, soon to be the guiding force behind the 'final solution', wrote with admiration about 'what Luther said and wrote about the Jews. No judgment could be sharper'.[41]

As for the Lutheran clergy, from early days substantial numbers of Lutheran clergy were ardent supporters of Hitler and of his anti-Semitism. In 1933, soon after Hitler had become Chancellor of Germany, Paul Althaus, professor and president of the prestigious Luther Society, hailed the Nazi victory 'as a gift and miracle of God'.[42]

In 1937 the prominent Lutheran theologian Wolf Meyer-Erlach published *Jews, Monks, and Luther* in which he identified Jews as 'an incessant army of demons', and hailed the Nazi Party as the 'fulfillment' of Luther's plans for the Jews.[43]

On 17 December 1941, seven Lutheran regional church confederations issued a statement in support of the Nazi state policy that in public all Jews must wear a yellow badge, asserting that 'since after his bitter experience Luther had suggested preventive measures against the Jews and their expulsion from German territory'.[44]

In his magisterial *The Reformation*, Diarmaid MacCulloch was quite correct that 'Luther's writing of 1543 is a blueprint for the Nazi's *Kristallnacht* of 1938',[45] when paramilitary Nazi forces smashed and burned Jewish synagogues, stores, hospitals, schools and homes throughout Germany and Austria. This was called 'Crystal Night' because of the shards of glass from broken windows that littered the streets in Jewish areas. In all, more than a thousand synagogues were burned that night. In response, Martin Sasse, a bishop of the Evangelical Lutheran Church who had joined the Nazi Party in 1930, applauded this event. He wrote 'On 10 November 1938, on Luther's birthday, the synagogues in Germany are burning'. This was most fitting and 'As Protestant Christians we fully recognize the great debt of gratitude we owe to Luther and we feel it our duty to warn all Protestant Christians in the whole world against the Jews and their protectors with Luther's very words.'[46]

Of course, many Lutheran clergy recognized the Nazis as evil and did their best to resist – some of them even giving their lives to that cause. But very substantial numbers strongly backed Hitler and his anti-Semitic policies, often citing Martin Luther as their guide. This was also reflected in the Lutheran rank and file; Hitler received a far higher percentage of the votes in 'Protestant' than in Catholic districts.[47]

Whatever the twentieth-century consequences of Luther's anti-Semitism, it greatly reinforced the prevalent anti-Semitism of the sixteenth century. Wherever Lutheran state churches arose, the Jews were expelled. Of course, these Lutherans expelled or persecuted members of every other brand of Christianity as well.

To sum up: the Reformations resulted in state churches that were even more repressive of individuals than the Catholic Church ever attempted to be. The Reformations did not contribute anything to religious freedom and tolerance; to the contrary. Finally, Martin Luther's vicious anti-Semitism played a significant role in legitimating the Holocaust, just as William Shirer claimed.

3

The misfortune of nationalistic states

This chapter does not mourn the collapse of Christendom, although it is hard not to be nostalgic for its many virtues, especially for the international character of the elite who ruled both its political and religious institutions. What this chapter mourns is the replacement of Christendom by powerful nation states, each with a distinctive and nationalistic culture. The Reformation played a potent role in this transformation. First, by subjugating the Church to the state, thereby eliminating the internationalism of religion – this also happened in Catholic nations. Second, by stimulating the creation of divisive national cultures. Among the consequences were far more brutal and extensive wars.

Christendom

Christendom slowly arose from the ashes of the Roman Empire and rested on the political disunity of Europe – as late as the fourteenth century there were more than a thousand independent political units[1] in the area now known as Europe, some so small that they are best referred to as *statelets*. Spanning this entire array of medieval states and statelets was a comprehensive Church structure based on geographic units – parishes and dioceses, united and ruled respectively by pastors and by bishops, under the direction of the Vatican. In each state and statelet there were close ties between the political and Church elites; often they were members of the same family – 75 per cent of medieval ascetic saints were from the nobility, 22 per cent of these from royalty.[2] Moreover, since all education was provided by the Church, all educated members of the ruling elites had been tutored by monks or clergy, often in Latin, and therefore nobility and clergy shared a common culture, even to their tastes in literature, music, art and architecture. This became even more pronounced after the founding of universities, beginning in the eleventh century, not because the nobility attended, but because their tutors did. Having a common culture and language facilitated interstate ties – intermarriages, and even the importation of 'foreigners' to replace heirless nobility, were common. Finally, all of the nobility answered to personal confessors, as was discussed in Chapter 1. Thus, the Continent was given moral and cultural unity, as well as some degree of political cohesion, by the Church. This was Christendom.

On medieval warfare

The most persistent and misleading myth about medieval European societies is that they lived in a state of constant, bloody warfare.[3] In truth, war was not so common and seldom bloody. For one thing, relatively small forces were involved – at the Battle of Hastings (in 1066), which resulted in the Norman conquest of England, about 10,000 Normans overcame about 7,000 English (the population of England was about 2.5 million at that time). The 'big' wars were seldom among Europeans, but involved fighting off external threats from invaders such as the Muslims, the Magyars and the Mongols. Moreover, these wars of resistance reflected the unity of Christendom in that many states often combined their forces.

It is quite true that medieval Europe consisted of warrior states, in that they were organized on military lines, and headed at each level by warrior knights. The basis of this governing structure was to protect residents from bandits and raiders (such as the Vikings before they became Europeans). Of course, given warrior rule, conflicts – whether based on territorial disputes, greed or personal affronts – tended to take military form. Nevertheless, the successful rulers (be they kings, princes or merely local barons) 'assiduously avoided battle'.[4] Although sometimes a war lasted for decades, 'in many years there were no battles'.[5] As Sir Charles Oman explained, 'the main reason [for so] few engagements in the open field is that the weaker side was always tempted to take shelter behind its walls rather than to offer battle'.[6] In a sense, this was an Age of Castles, not an Age of Battles. Except, of course for the Crusades, which involved large forces of knights from many parts of Europe who marched several thousand miles to fight, and usually win, many pitched battles against far larger Muslim forces. As Mark Greengrass put it, the 'Crusades became Western Christendom's most ambitious project'.[7]

The Christendom Crusades

On 27 November 1095, Pope Urban II mounted a platform set up in a meadow outside the French city of Clermont, surrounded in all directions by a huge crowd. A vigorous man of 53, Urban was blessed with an unusually powerful and expressive voice that made it possible for him to be heard at a great distance. On this occasion, he gave the speech that launched the First Crusade.

Contrary to the views of recent Western apologists, the Crusades were not the start of European colonialism, meant to gain lands and loot from the Muslim Middle East. They were a defensive response to the latest in many centuries of Muslim attempts to colonize the West. Keep in mind that the Battle of Tours (in 732), wherein an army of Franks defeated a large Muslim force, was fought only about 120 miles south of Paris. At that time Muslims already occupied Spain and southern Italy, having previously swept over all of Christian North Africa. Subsequently, they attempted repeatedly to invade Europe from the east – up through Greece and into Hungary. The First Crusade was organized in response to an appeal from the Emperor of Byzantium to send help to repel the Seljuk Turks, who had conquered Jerusalem and then driven to within 100 miles of Constantinople.

There were many reasons why the pope and Europe's nobility might have ignored a plea for help from Byzantium. For one thing, the Western cultural heritage and its Christianity were Roman, while the Byzantines were Greeks, whose lifestyle seemed decadent to Europeans and whose 'Orthodox' Christianity held Roman Catholicism in contempt – often persecuting its priests and practitioners. Nevertheless, Pope Urban thought it far more important to push back against Muslim imperialism than to hold grudges against Byzantium. Moreover, he meant not only to come to the aid of Byzantium, but to go all the way and liberate Jerusalem, thus ending the newly arisen brutalization of Christian pilgrims. Therefore, he organized a huge Church council at Clermont and gave his famous speech, concluding: 'If you are conquered, you will have the glory of dying in the very same place as Jesus Christ, and God will never forget that he found you in the holy battalions.'[8] Now, shouts of '*Dieu le volt!*' spread through the crowd, as knights and nobles swore that next year they would set out to liberate the Holy Land. And they did.

Even so, the First Crusade probably would not have come to pass had the pope left things in the hands of the knights who were in his audience at Clermont. The crusade took place because the pope was able to recruit hundreds (perhaps thousands) to preach it all across Europe. Indeed, the pope himself spent the next nine months travelling more than two thousand miles preaching the crusade. And while the pope toured:

> papal letters and legates travelled swiftly to England, Normandy, and Flanders, to Genoa and Bologna, exhorting, commanding, and persuading . . . Later in the same year the pope sent the bishops of Orange and Grenoble to preach the crusade in Genoa, and bring the formidable Genoese sea-power into the war.[9]

Eventually, five major armies of crusaders were enlisted under the leadership of five princes.

King Philip I of France wanted to lead a crusader army, but he could not, having been excommunicated for marrying another man's wife without either of them obtaining a divorce. So his brother Hugh, Count of Vermandois, raised an army of noble knights from the area around Paris and, joined by a large contingent of German knights, set out for Constantinople in August 1096.

Godfrey of Bouillon (in what is today Belgium), who was also Duke of Lower Lorraine (a German-speaking state), sold most of his property to go crusading. He was accompanied by his brothers Eustace III and Baldwin of Boulogne, who took along his Norman wife, Godehilde of Toeni. This large army also left in August 1096.

Bohemond, Prince of Taranto, representing the Norman Kingdom of Italy and Sicily, organized and led what may well have been the most fearsome force of them all, made up entirely of Norman veterans of many campaigns. They sailed from Bari in October and landed on the Bulgarian coast, marching from there to Constantinople.

The fourth army of crusaders was recruited and led by Raymond IV of Toulouse in south-western France. He also departed in October at the head of a force that included some Spanish knights – he was accompanied by his third wife who was the daughter of King Alfonso VI of Castile.

Finally, Robert, Duke of Normandy, was the eldest son of William the Conqueror who had been disowned by his father for plotting against him with the King of France. To obtain the funds needed to raise and sustain a crusader army, Robert mortgaged Normandy to his brother King William of England. The duke's forces were made up of knights from England and Scotland as well as from Normandy (plus a few from Denmark) and also included his cousin, Robert II, Count of Flanders, and his brother-in-law Stephen, Count of Blois.

The Second Crusade took place about 50 years after the First and was equally international in its make-up. King Louis VII of France joined forces with the German King Conrad III, thereby uniting the two most powerful monarchies in Europe. The Third Crusade was led by the King of England, known as Richard the Lionheart, by King Philip II of France, and by Frederick I (Frederick Barbarossa), King of Germany and Italy.

Clearly, the Crusades demonstrated that Christendom was a reality. Despite their various internal wars, the European elite saw themselves as members of a community.

Intellectual life

But Christendom was not merely a community of warriors or even a community of the nobility. It was a civilization! Unfortunately, for generations everyone was taught that the era beginning with the fall of Rome and ending not long before the Reformations was correctly known as the 'Dark Ages'. Nonsense. This was an era of remarkable progress in technology, high culture and even in morality – so much so that when Columbus sailed, 25 years before Luther nailed up his theses, Europe was far ahead of the rest of the world. I have written on this at great length elsewhere. It is unnecessary here to discuss the immense technological progress of this era – from horse collars to printing presses. But I will note several aspects of the intellectual life of Christendom.

Western orchestral music is far more complex in its instrumentation and harmonies by comparison with non-European and some popular music forms, and it also differs by being fully scored. This was not something that began in the eighteenth century, in the 'classical' era of Mozart and Haydn, but was well along by the thirteenth century. In fact, polyphonic music, the simultaneous sounding of two or more musical lines – hence harmonies, dates from as early as the ninth century (the Greeks and Romans had only monophonic music). And an adequate system of written musical notation was developed by the tenth century. This meant that musicians could play music without having first heard it played and that compositions could last across the generations and spread easily from place to place. Thus, in medieval times, as later, music was entirely international – the elites all across Europe enjoyed the same music. They heard it in church and at concerts given for the nobility at court.

The magnificent 'Gothic' cathedrals that exist all across Europe – from Scandinavia to Portugal, from England to Poland – also testify to the unity of Christendom. Of course, they were not built by the barbarous Goths – that label was imposed on them by snobs during the so-called Enlightenment, who scorned these buildings for not conforming to 'the standards of classical Greece and Rome:

"May he who invented [this style of architecture] be cursed."[10] Having had no knowledge of the flying buttress, which made it possible for the first time to erect tall buildings with thin walls, the Greeks and Romans could not have built anything like these cathedrals. But medieval Europeans could and did – and perhaps nothing has equalled them since.

Architecture and music were marvellous decorations on elite life in Christendom, but this remarkable civilization – and the rise of science that it was incubating – rested on a singular Christian invention: the university. 'Universities, like cathedrals . . . are a product of the Middle Ages.'[11]

The word 'university' is a shortened version of the Latin *universitas magistrorum et scholarium*, or 'community of teachers and scholars'. This new institution developed from cathedral schools that served to train priests and it was specifically meant to be more advanced, to impart 'higher learning'. The first university was founded in Bologna, in northern Italy, in about 1088. Next came the University of Paris in 1150, Oxford in 1167, Palencia in 1208, and Cambridge in 1209. Twenty-four others followed before the end of the fourteenth century and at least 28 more were founded during the following century, including one as far north as Uppsala in Sweden in 1477. These were not small places consisting of a few masters and several hundred students. By the year 1200, only 50 years after its founding, the University of Paris is estimated to have had as many as 5,000 students and several hundred faculty.[12] Many students came long distances to enrol and a surprising number moved from one university to another – switching between Oxford and Paris was common. Student movement was facilitated by the fact that there were no language barriers: all instruction, everywhere, was in Latin.

Faculty also moved from one university to another amazingly often. Then, as today, one gained fame and invitations to join other faculties by *innovation*. It was not who knew Aristotle word for word, but who had found errors in Aristotle. Thus, from the start, some university faculty devoted themselves to the pursuit of new knowledge, thereby launching the rise of science as will be discussed at length in Chapter 5. The university also provided an institutional base for the pursuit of theology – the University of Paris was home to Thomas Aquinas in the thirteenth century and John Calvin was a student there in the sixteenth.

Universities quickly transformed Church leadership. By the thirteenth century nearly half of the highest offices in the Church (those of abbot, archbishop and cardinal) were held by men who had earned master's degrees. And, since the same curriculum was followed by all universities, all educated Europeans shared a common intellectual background.

And then it ended!

For Europe's elites, 'the Reformation replaced loyalty to Christendom with loyalty to "nation", and it also replaced Christian identity with national identity'.[13] In doing so, the Reformations 'dissolved much of the intellectual and moral cement which had long held Europeans together'.[14] From this came the nationalistic state filled with patriotic citizens, ready to fight for their nation's destiny.

We already have seen in Chapters 1 and 2 that the Reformations led to the establishment of state churches in 'Protestant' nations, while those nations that remained Catholic already had the functional equivalent of state churches in that the kings appointed the top Church officials in their nations. In this manner, the religious counterbalance to the secular leaders that had characterized Christendom disappeared along with the international outlook and culture associated with the Church. Europe now became a continent of locals, both culturally and politically.

Building national cultures

In a sense, national cultures long predated the Reformations, lying underneath the international layer of the elite culture of Christendom. 'Across the landmass of western Europe . . . lay thousands of villages and parishes, their inhabitants . . . suspicious . . . towards the cosmopolitan ambitions and bureaucracy of the international order.'[15] And the cultures that prevailed in these places were local as to customs, outlook and especially language. With the breakdown of Christendom, the political elite in each nation became increasingly localized in all these aspects. Indeed, this localization was speeded and empowered by the Reformations, especially in terms of language.

When Luther was born, very few Europeans other than some monks, nuns and clergy were literate, mainly because there was almost nothing to read in the language they spoke. Hand-copied books were too precious to be available to the masses and, besides, they all were written in Latin. That changed suddenly and dramatically. On the eve of the German Reformation:

> printing presses existed in over two hundred [European] cities and towns. An estimated six million books had been printed and half of the thirty thousand titles were on religious subjects. More books were printed in the forty years between 1460 and 1500 than had been produced by scribes and monks throughout the entire Middle Ages.[16]

Even so, this was but a trickle compared with the flood of books produced by the Reformation in Germany alone. By the time of Luther's death it is estimated that a million copies of the Bible in German had been printed.[17] And, because Luther wrote so magnificently in German, many believe that his huge literary output, and especially his translation of the Bible (1534), greatly shaped modern, written German.[18] It certainly is true that the King James Version of the Bible (which appeared in 1611) has done the same for writers in English (myself included). However, an earlier English translation had appeared in 1538, marking the break with Latin. In 1524 the New Testament was translated into Danish, a Dutch translation of the whole Bible was printed in 1526, a French translation appeared in Antwerp in 1530, a Swedish version in 1541, a Czech translation in 1549, a Polish translation in 1563, and a Spanish translation in 1569 – by 1600 there probably were translations of the Bible into every European language. Not only were Bibles now readable in one's native language, but they were available to be read – prior to the printing press even few cathedrals, let alone parish churches, possessed a Bible. The plentiful existence of Bibles in every European language established each as a written, literary language.

Of course, many books besides Bibles were being rushed into print as the reading public exploded in size – unmentioned in most histories of printing is that pornography was an early bestseller.[19] What truly mattered was that now local writers began to produce books for the local market, often focused on local legends and with local themes. Soon there was a remarkable and revered 'literature' in each national language – by such 'literary lions' as Shakespeare, Goethe, Molière and Cervantes. Of major importance were localized histories that stressed the unique heritage and external conflicts of the nation's past – some actual, some of them fanciful. For example, in England stories of the (perhaps) fictional King Arthur combined with the remarkable exploits of the real Richard the Lionheart to help produce a national literary heritage. In France, the story of Jeanne d'Arc, how she had rallied the French forces and then died a martyr's death at the hands of the hated English, provided a central core for a national 'history' celebrating French superiority. Although they lacked national political unity, German writers soon created a national culture, beginning with Jakob Wimpfeling's claim in 1505 that Charlemagne had not been a Frenchman, but had really been a German ruling over the French.[20] From this beginning, a German historical 'memory' soon included a host of legendary figures eventually to be enshrined in Wagnerian operas.

The creation of distinctive national cultures was reinforced by the nationalization of university life. In the wake of the Reformations and the publishing explosion, universities ceased to teach in Latin. Now, to study at Paris, students needed to speak and read French and should they wish to transfer to Cambridge they had to know English as well. The same was true for faculty. Soon, universities began to celebrate their different national cultures and to stress the glory of their national histories. This was greatly encouraged by policies of exclusion. Thus, in Scandinavia no one could enter a nation, let alone enrol at a local university, unless one belonged to the state church. Only members in good standing of the Church of England could enrol in Oxford or Cambridge. Only Catholics could attend the University of Paris. And so it went.

The major consequence of all this was the creation of distinctive national cultures that were embraced at all levels of society. That is, the upper-class as well as the lower-class French became distinctively French and noticeably different from the upper- and lower-class English or Germans. Moreover, most people in each of these nations were fully aware of these differences and proud of them, regarding their culture as superior to all others.

The rise of nationalism

'Nationalism' has become a much overused term, subject to far too many and often muddled definitions.[21] But it is the best word for identifying one of the central facts of modern life, having to do with the bond between individuals and their community of residence. I will give little attention to the form of nationalism exhibited by members of an internal minority wishing to possess their own state, such as the Basques within Spain. I will attend to nationalism involving nations wishing to form independent states, but my main focus will be on the form of nationalism that involves *patriotism*, defined as *deep loyalty to the nation state of residence.*

As suggested by this definition, not all nations are states and not all states are nations. States are political units governing a geographic area. Nations are geo-cultural units, an area wherein the population has a sense of common identity including a language and a distinct culture. Some states include a number of nations – modern Britain, for example, includes the nations of England, Scotland and Wales. Obviously, then, some nations are not states. A nation state is both – a political unit whose residents share a common culture. Historically, England was long a nation state and Scotland has been one from time to time. In any event, the nationalism I wish to examine consists of the patriotism generated by the nation state or by a nation that becomes a nation state.

How, then, did nationalism arise?

The first step was the existence of multiple states in proximity and with distinctive cultures. States existed within Christendom, but they were ruled by elites having an interstate culture. The Reformations shattered that culture. The formation of state churches greatly facilitated the development of distinctive local cultures – everyone was, or was supposed to be, of the same religion. The development of national cultures was encouraged by the linguistic and 'ethnic' homogeneity of these states. In part this was a function of the 'tribal' past of Europe and in part it was a result of exclusion and/or repression. That is, Europe was peopled by descendants of a whole host of ethnic settlers and invaders – Anglo-Saxons, Goths, Franks, Huns and the like. These groups had settled in specific places and retained important aspects of their original cultures, especially language – although some shifted to a language that was, in effect, a rather simplified form of Latin (the so-called Romance languages of French, Spanish and Italian). The rise of states following the collapse of the Roman Empire tended to reflect these ethnic settlements. In addition, the absolute rulers of the states that arose from 'Protestantism' often did the equivalent of 'ethnic cleansing'. Foreigners were simply excluded and driven out of the Scandinavian nation states. In 'Germany', laws prohibiting Catholics or 'Protestants' from living in various princedoms resulted in selective migration. In France, the repression of the Protestant Huguenots produced an effective homogeneity. England repressed Catholics into virtual invisibility and submerged Scottish and Welsh influences. As will be seen, many culturally homogeneous European nation states came into being during the nineteenth century through wars of independence.

Another factor was that the nation states of Europe are closely packed. France borders Belgium, Germany, Switzerland, Italy and Spain and is less than 30 miles across the Channel from England. Such proximity not only has been a constant source of conflict over borders, but has encouraged the more powerful nation states to attempt to incorporate the weaker ones. Proximity also exacerbated cultural conflicts and contempt, in that neighbours have been very aware of cultural differences and insults. Thus, as early as 1577 William Harrison's *Description of England* set a new tone 'in which the liberties and noble character of the English nation were contrasted with the dissolute and depraved manners of the French'.[22] And so it continued. In the nineteenth century the English referred to condoms as *French letters*, while the French referred to them as *capotes anglaises*. While the French were emphatic that theirs was by far the superior literary language in Europe, the English were fond of noting that either the French could not pronounce their own language or they could not spell.

National cultures continued to develop for centuries, some within nation states, others as nations within states. Then came two major developments. First was the French Revolution. Second, the nineteenth century was marked by wars of independence, many of which failed, but some established new nation states, all of their citizens brimming with nationalistic fervour.

The French Revolution was a mass movement against the ruling elite. In January 1793, King Louis XVI was beheaded, soon to be followed by 16,594 victims in Paris (including Queen Marie Antoinette and all the other nobles who could be apprehended) and another 25,000 elsewhere in France. Believing that now the nation was theirs, the French people embraced a level of nationalism previously unknown. This resulted in a 'nation-in-arms', at war to spread the revolutionary doctrine of 'liberty, equality and fraternity'. French nationalism, in turn, generated nationalistic responses in other European nations, as will be seen.

European wars of independence began in 1804 with the Serbian breakaway from the Ottoman Empire. Twenty years later the Greeks followed suit, also gaining independence from the Ottomans. In 1830, the Belgians revolted and gained their independence from the Netherlands. Mid-century nationalist revolts in Poland and Hungary failed. In 1867, Hungary gained autonomy. In 1878, Serbia, Romania and Montenegro won their independence. Norway broke away from Sweden in 1905, Bulgarians gained their freedom in 1908, and Albania became independent in 1912.

This wave of nation-state creation was in tune with the remarkable artistic era known as Romanticism, which celebrated heroic nationalism. Musicians, writers, artists and even philosophers drew upon national folklore to idealize their nation's cultural heritage. Thus, the German philosopher G. W. F. Hegel (1770–1831) claimed that every historical era is dominated by a zeitgeist, or spirit of the age, which determined which nation determined history at that time. Because of Luther, Hegel believed that the zeitgeist had settled on the German people in his time. Others celebrated the French Revolution. Perhaps the leading Romantic musician was Richard Wagner (1813–83), the German opera composer, who believed there were distinct musical styles inherent in every national culture that outsiders could not fully comprehend, claiming that therefore the Jews in Germany could not really appreciate German music. Wagner's music was beloved by Hitler.

Nationalism and conflict

Unlike most who write on the subject, I do not find nationalism deplorable. Neither do I find it on the wane – the recent opposition to the European Union that has burst forth in many nations (such as the recent British exit) surely suggests that local majorities resent and reject the attempt to submerge national independence beneath a continental bureaucracy. There is nothing inherently wicked or ignorant about nationalism – about pride in one's culture and history and a preference for one's way of life.[23] That said, the fact remains that nationalism can generate and worsen conflicts between nations – and in the nineteenth and twentieth centuries it did so.

It all began with the French Revolution. Prior to that, in the seventeenth and eighteenth centuries European warfare had involved very small professional armies, fighting very circumscribed campaigns having almost no impact on civilian life. In 1643, the entire Prussian army consisted of 5,500 professional soldiers. A century later the fierce Prussian army commanded by Frederick the Great numbered only 90,000 and still triumphed in the Seven Years War (1756–63) against France, Austria and Russia.

Then, in 1792, the National Convention of the French Revolution passed legislation calling for a '*levée en masse*', making all young men subject to conscription into the army. The legislation read: 'Any Frenchman is a soldier and owes himself to the defense of the nation', thus assuming patriotism.[24] Within the year the Grande Armée numbered 500,000 and the French smashed the Prussians and others, outnumbering them on the battlefield often by as much as ten to one. Between 1800 and 1813, more than 2.6 million young men were drafted into the French army.[25] Of course, the rest of Europe had to respond. So one nation after another instituted universal conscription, until only England (safe behind its Channel barrier) had not done so.

As a result, by the time Napoleon Bonaparte took command of the huge French army, he confronted large, conscripted Austrian, Prussian and Russian armies. Worse yet, these mass armies were no longer made up of paid professionals who fought with restraint and caution. Now they consisted of relatively naive and youthful masses, expected to do their duty as defined by the state.

Of course, casualties soared. The number killed in one battle often far exceeded the total number of troops involved in an entire war a century earlier – the French lost nearly 30,000 men, including 49 generals, when they *won* the Battle of Borodino, 75 miles from Moscow! All told, Napoleon probably lost 400,000 men in his effort to defeat Russia.

Only highly nationalistic states could successfully impose mandatory conscription on their populations. Only highly nationalistic cultures could make people willing to die for their country. Consequently, nationalism was a major factor in the catastrophic wars of the twentieth century.[26]

The First World War: 1914–1918

The proximate cause of the war was Serbian nationalism. Austrian Archduke Franz Ferdinand, heir to the throne of Austria-Hungary, was assassinated by a Serbian nationalist on 28 June 1914. Anti-Serbian riots led to a declaration of war on Serbia by Austria-Hungary, and Europe's major powers joined in based on their treaty obligations.

That nationalism played a major role in causing and sustaining what became the most devastating European war up to that time is revealed by the joyful crowds that celebrated its beginning. 'In the capitals of the belligerent powers people danced in the streets and garlanded the departing troops with flowers . . .'[27] There is a famous picture of 25-year-old Adolf Hitler in a Munich crowd cheering the start of the war (he later served with distinction in the German army). As Ernst Jünger recalled: 'We were enraptured by the war. We had set out in a rain of flowers, in a drunken atmosphere of blood and roses.'[28]

Then, to fully ratify their absolute commitment to their nations, Europeans engaged in an orgy of nationalistic name changing. In Germany, the Hotel Westminster became the Hotel Lindendorf, and the Café Piccadilly was changed to Café Vaterland. In Paris, the Rue d'Allemagne became the Rue Jean Jaurès. The British royal family changed its name from the House of Saxe-Coburg and Gotha to the House of Windsor, the noble Battenbergs became the Mountbattens, and many other British families with German-sounding names changed them too. The breed of dogs known as the German Shepherd was changed to the Alsatian by the English Kennel Club (it was changed back in 1977), and after they entered the war, Americans renamed Dachshunds as Liberty Pups. The city of Berlin, in Ontario, Canada changed its name to Kitchener, after the famous British general Lord Kitchener. In Chicago, Lubeck, Frankfort and Hamburg streets were renamed Dickens, Charleston and Shakespeare. And Americans stopped referring to Sauerkraut, instead calling it Liberty Cabbage. As Hagen Schulze noted: 'Bizarre details of this kind may seem trivial, but they indicate a degree of national fervour such as had never been known in previous wars.'[29]

It also was war on a scale that had never been known before. In the whole of Europe, only four nations, Denmark, Luxembourg, Norway and Sweden, stayed out. Beyond Europe, Australia, Canada, India, New Zealand, South Africa, the United States and the Ottoman Empire also took part in the war. A total of 8 million soldiers died in battle and another 2 million of other causes. In addition, millions more were severely handicapped by their wounds. As for civilians, more than 2 million died as a result of military actions or were murdered by invaders.

When it was over, the major governments on both sides were bankrupt and millions of women never married due to the shortage of young men. But nationalism was not only undiminished, but greatly exacerbated. Early on this was manifested in two important ways. First, the peace treaty imposed staggering 'reparations' upon the defeated nations, creating deep feelings of grievance and hatred that played a very substantial role in causing a resumption of war a generation later. Second, the doctrine of self-determination imposed on the defeated nations (particularly through the urging of the American president) used local nationalistic sentiments to justify stripping away many former European provinces from the losers by making them independent states: Albania, Finland, Czechoslovakia, Yugoslavia, Poland, Hungary, Latvia, Lithuania and Estonia – and the relatively small nation of Austria – was all that was left from the dismembered Austro-Hungarian Empire.

The desire to reclaim some of these lost areas played an important role in causing the Second World War. Worse yet, the economic suffering not only in the defeated nations, but in many of those that had been newly created to suit local nationalist sentiments and without regard for economic realities, made for widespread vulnerability to the rise of dictatorships. Russia had succumbed even before the end of the First World War with the rise to power of Lenin and the Bolsheviks in 1917. In 1922 Benito Mussolini seized power in Italy – a year later dictatorships were established in Bulgaria, Spain and Turkey. In 1925 a dictatorship arose in Albania; in 1926 the same occurred in Poland, Portugal and Lithuania. In 1929 a dictator came to power in Yugoslavia, and in 1930 in Romania. Hitler took absolute control of Germany in 1933. In 1934 Estonia and Latvia became dictatorships, and in 1936 Greece did too. That same year a new dictator overcame the leftist tyrants and took charge in Spain. Hence, in 1939 17 of the 28 European nations were ruled by dictators who emphasized nationalism and many of whom seemed ready for war.

The Second World War: 1939–1945

There was no dancing in the streets at the outbreak of the Second World War, when Germany invaded Poland on 1 September 1939. But nationalism remained a major factor. Playing on German grievances vis-à-vis the First World War peace treaty, Hitler had risen to power with promises to restore national honour and regain lost territories, but above all with his celebration of the supreme national character of Germany. Keep in mind that 'Nazi' is an acronym for National Socialist, and Hitler redefined the concept of German nationality to the level of race – authentic Germans belonged to the Aryan or Nordic 'master race', with a biological right to rule. It was relatively easy for Hitler to make these claims given the existing 'fantastic idealization of the German character, of the virtues, language, the culture and the achievement of the Germans'[30] dating from the sixteenth century, first proposed by the humanists and then strongly reinforced by Luther, who anticipated Hitler in excluding the Jews from belonging to the German nation. As was seen in Chapter 2, Luther preceded Hitler by four centuries in condemning the 'evil, corrupt, and traitorous Jewish race', to which Hitler added the Slavic *Untermenschen* (subhuman 'undermen'). Similar ideas were popular in many parts of Europe. In fact, anti-Semitism was widespread in England at the time, and Franklin D. Roosevelt refused to let boatloads of Jews attempting to escape from Europe land in the United States. Nor should we forget that the Jews in France were not rounded up and shipped off to the death camps by Germans – that was done by the French police.

In the end, the Second World War made the First World War seem like a minor engagement. Military deaths totalled about 21 million and, with the massive bombing of cities as well as street-to-street fighting in hundreds of cities, about 27 million civilians died as well – not counting the millions murdered in the Nazi death camps!

Sad to say, all of this can be traced back, at least in part, to the destruction of Christendom which was accomplished by the Reformations.

4

The myth of the Protestant Ethic

> A glance at the occupational statistics of any country of mixed religious composition brings to light with remarkable frequency . . . the fact that business leaders and owners of capital, as well as the higher grades of skilled labour, and even more the higher technically and commercially trained personnel of modern enterprises, are overwhelmingly Protestant.

With that sentence Max Weber (1864–1920) began one of the most famous works of sociology ever written.

Die Protestantische Ethik und der Geist des Kapitalismus was first published in German as two essays in 1904–5, and was translated into English and published in 1930 as a book: *The Protestant Ethic and the Spirit of Capitalism.* As suggested by the title, Weber proposed to explain why it was that industrial capitalism originated, and tended to flourish, only in Protestant areas or nations. His answer: because Protestantism caused people to work hard and live frugally. Weber identified this as the 'Protestant Ethic'.

Weber claimed that industrial capitalism required more than greed and the desire to increase one's wealth – these are universal human traits. Rather, what was special about industrial capitalism was that it required people to combine their efforts to gain wealth with frugality and this allowed them to reinvest the maximum amount of their profits in order to acquire ever greater wealth. Weber called this the 'Spirit of Capitalism'. He then asked, how did the Protestant Ethic and the Spirit of Capitalism come to be linked?

The first step, according to Weber, was Luther's designation of work as a divine calling: as 'a task set by God . . . The only way of living acceptably to God was not to surpass worldly morality in monastic asceticism, but solely through the fulfillment of the obligations imposed upon the individual by his position in the world. That was his calling.'[1] Weber went on to note that 'this moral justification of worldly activity was one of the most important results of the Reformation, especially of Luther's part in it'. Moreover, this conception of work does not exist among 'Catholic peoples nor those of classical antiquity . . . while [it is found among] all predominantly Protestant peoples'.[2]

By itself, however, to regard work as a divine calling probably would not have been sufficient to produce capitalism. In addition, it was necessary that people pursue their calling with extreme effort. To explain this level of motivation, Weber turned to Calvinism and the notion of divine election. While Lutherans and Catholics disagree as to how one earns salvation – through faith alone or through faith and works – Calvin taught that one can do nothing whatever to gain salvation. According to Calvin's doctrine of predestination, God determines that some are elect (saved) and most people are damned on a basis known only to God, and that's it. Nothing one can do in this life changes one's fate.

Weber proposed that 'the decisive problem is: How was this doctrine borne?' How could people live with this uncertainty as to their unchangeable fate? As he put it: 'The question, Am I one of the elect? must sooner or later have arisen for every believer and forced all other interests into the background.'[3] To this, Calvinism proposed two responses. First, 'it is held to be an absolute duty to consider oneself chosen, and to combat all doubts as temptations of the devil, since lack of self-confidence is the result of insufficient faith.'[4] But it was the second response that Weber regarded as the basis for capitalism: 'to attain certainty in one's own election and justification in the daily struggle of life'[5] by achieving worldly success. That is, 'faith had to be proved by its objective results'.[6] Thus, 'the God of Calvinism demanded of his believers not single good works, but a life of good works'.[7] Hence, 'now every Christian had to be a monk all his life [but to do so] within mundane occupations. But . . . Calvinism added something positive to this, the idea of the necessity of proving one's faith in worldly activity'.[8]

Thus, the need to be reassured that one was saved, and to demonstrate that fact to others, required dedication to achieving maximum worldly success. One did this by rejecting 'idleness and temptations of the flesh . . . not leisure and enjoyment, but only activity serves to increase the glory of God'.[9] From this perspective, 'waste of time is the first and in principle the deadliest of sins'.[10] Weber identified this as the fully developed *Protestant Ethic*. And, according to him, this ethic subsequently manifested itself in the *Spirit of Capitalism*, which spurns consumption in favour of the reinvestment of wealth to increase one's means of production. As he put it:

> the religious valuation of restless, continuous, systematic work in a worldly calling, as the highest means to asceticism, and at the same time the surest and most evident proof of rebirth and genuine faith, must have been the most powerful conceivable lever for the expansion of that attitude toward life which we have here called the spirit of capitalism.[11]

Thus, Weber argued, the rise of industrial capitalism was a result of the Reformations, especially of Calvinism.

Weber's thesis is now more than a century old and nearly all of the introductory sociology textbooks (but not mine) take it to be a settled fact that the rise of industrial capitalism took place initially in predominantly Protestant countries and that within nations having both Protestants and Catholics, the Protestants dominated the capitalist economy. Moreover, a number of sociologists have attempted to account for the modernization of various non-Western societies by 'finding' an equivalent of the Protestant Ethic in their local religions[12] – Robert Bellah claimed that such an ethic existed in Japan's forms of Buddhism, Confucianism and Shinto during the Tokugawa era.[13]

Nevertheless, it's all a myth!

Weber's starting assumption, stated in his first sentence, that there is a strong link between Protestantism and capitalism is false. Hence, there was nothing that needed to be explained.

Contrary evidence

There is by now such a mountain of published research (supposedly) based on Weber's Protestant Ethic thesis that it would take many weeks to locate most of it, let alone read it. Fortunately, most of it has little or no relevance to Weber's actual thesis and is so silly (comparing Protestant and Catholic student grades in accounting courses) and/or tendentious (does the Protestant Ethic make high school students insensitive to the plight of the poor?) it need not be read. Moreover, in this pile of publications there is rarely any evidence that is even vaguely pertinent to Weber's actual thesis. Nor did Weber offer any, having been content to quote Benjamin Franklin for examples of the spirit of capitalism and to otherwise rely on anecdotes.

Nevertheless, from the very start there have been devastating refutations of Weber's thesis based on appropriate evidence. Possibly the first of these empirical refutations was by a fellow German, Felix Rachfahl (1867–1925), published four years after Weber's original essays had appeared in German. Rachfahl noted that the Protestant Ethic thesis was contradicted by the geography of the rise of industrial capitalism. For example, Amsterdam and Antwerp developed industrial capitalism very early when both were Catholic cities, while the Protestant Scandinavian cities were very late to develop industrial capitalism. Of course, Rachfahl weakened his case against Weber's thesis by agreeing that Protestantism far exceeded Catholicism in terms of having a higher standard of morality. Next came another German economist, Lujo Brentano (1844–1931), who correctly noted that industrial capitalism originated in southern Europe long before the German Reformation and was taken north mainly by Catholic banking firms.

Then came the British economic historian R. H. Tawney (1880–1962) whose fine book *Religion and the Rise of Capitalism* (1926) reiterated in far greater detail that industrial capitalism began in the Catholic cities of southern Europe and that even when capitalism appeared in the north, it was at first controlled by Catholic bankers from the south. Tawney added an additional twist by suggesting that 'nascent capitalism ... [shaped] Calvinism's attitude to enterprise and the accumulation of wealth, not *vice versa*'.[14]

In 1933, another British historian, H. M. Robertson (1905–84), again demonstrated that the rise of capitalism long preceded the Reformations, being of Catholic origin. As for the Protestant Ethic, it was produced by an already capitalistic-minded middle class. There were more such rejections of Weber during the 1940s and early 1950s and then came a major study: Kurt Samuelsson (1921–2005) published *Religion and Economic Action: The Protestant Ethic, the Rise of Capitalism, and the Abuses of Scholarship* in Swedish in 1957 and an English translation appeared in 1961. In his review of the book, the great Harvard sociologist George C. Homans (1910–89) put it this way: Samuelsson does not 'just tinker with Weber's hypothesis, but leaves it in ruins'.[15] Samuelsson recited once again the wealth of evidence that the rise of industrial capitalism preceded the Reformations.

But Weber's thesis lived on in the textbooks and in a continuing flow of trivial so-called applications. So, in 1969 the famous British historian Hugh Trevor-Roper (1914–2003) took time to note that 'The idea that large-scale industrial capitalism was ideologically impossible before the Reformation is exploded by the simple fact that it existed'.[16] Ten years later the celebrated French historian Fernand Braudel (1902–85) complained that:

> all historians have opposed this tenuous theory [the Protestant Ethic] although they have not managed to get rid of it once and for all. Yet it is clearly false. The northern countries took over the place that earlier had been so long and brilliantly occupied by the old capitalist centers of the Mediterranean. They invented nothing, either in technology or business management.[17]

Nevertheless, in 1998 the members of the International Sociological Association voted Weber's *The Protestant Ethic and the Spirit of Capitalism* the fourth most important sociological book of the twentieth century. Many of us were shocked by the announcement and forced to wonder when and if sociology would ever become an empirical science. The announcement also prompted Jacques Delacroix and François Nielsen, two American sociologists born in Europe, to undertake a study to demonstrate with historical statistics that the Protestant Ethic thesis is, as they put it, merely a 'beloved academic myth'.[18]

The first task these scholars faced was to assemble data on the extent of industrial capitalism in the nations of Europe at as early a date as possible. Eventually they obtained data for Austria, Belgium, Denmark, Finland, France,

Germany, Great Britain, Ireland, Italy, the Netherlands, Norway, Portugal, Spain, Sweden and Switzerland. For each nation they determined the percentage of Protestants in the population at the middle of the nineteenth century. Then they located a number of measures of industrial development such as the percentage of the male labour force employed in industry and the extension of the railway networks. They also located financial measures such as wealth per capita, savings bank deposits per capita, and the year of founding of the principal stock exchange. Then they calculated the relationship between Protestantism and these measures of industrial capitalism. The results were zero: Catholic and Protestant nations did not differ!

Subsequently, a study published in 2011, using GDP per capita as well as growth of GDP per capita from as far back as 1500 for the 15 major European nations, found no significant correlation between Protestantism and the rise of industrial capitalism.[19] Finally, Davide Cantoni at Harvard managed to assemble data on growth from 1300 to 1900 for 272 German cities. After analysing the data he reported that Protestantism had no impact on economic growth.[20] So much, then, for the fourth best sociological book of the twentieth century.

Nevertheless, Weber wasn't entirely wrong. Religion did play a major role in the rise of capitalism. But, rather than being based on a Protestant Ethic, capitalism was a very Catholic invention: it first appeared in the great monastic estates, way back in the ninth century.

Monasticism and capitalism*

The Bible often condemns greed and wealth – 'For the love of money is the root of all evils'[21] – but it does not directly

---

*Portions of the next three sections have previously appeared in Stark, 2016.

condemn commerce or merchants. However, many of the very early Church fathers shared the views prevalent in the Greco-Roman world that commerce is a degrading activity and, at best, involves great moral risk – that it is very difficult to avoid sin in the course of buying and selling.[22] However, soon after the conversion of Constantine (312 BCE) the Church ceased to be dominated by ascetics and attitudes towards commerce began to mellow, leading Augustine to teach that wickedness was not inherent in commerce, but that, as with any occupation, it was up to the individual to live righteously.

Augustine also ruled that price was not simply a function of the seller's costs, but also of the buyer's desire for the item sold. In this way, Augustine gave legitimacy, not merely to merchants, but to the eventual deep involvement of the Church in the birth of capitalism when its earliest forms began to appear in about the ninth century in the great estates belonging to monastic orders. Because of the immense increases in agricultural productivity over the previous several centuries that resulted from such significant innovations as the switch from oxen to horses, the heavy mouldboard plough, and the three-field system, the monastic estates were no longer limited to mere subsistence agriculture. Instead, they began to specialize in particular crops or products and to sell these at a profit allowing them to purchase their other needs, which led them to initiate a cash economy. They also began to reinvest their profits to increase their productive capacity and, as their incomes continued to mount, this led many monasteries to become banks, lending to the nobility – as they did to so many crusaders. As Randall Collins noted, this was not merely a sort of 'proto' capitalism involving only the 'institutional preconditions for capitalism . . . but a version of the developed characteristics of capitalism itself'.[23] Collins referred to this as 'religious capitalism',[24] adding that the 'dynamism of the medieval economy was primarily that of the Church'.[25]

Throughout the medieval era, the Church was by far the largest landowner in Europe and its liquid assets and annual income far surpassed not only that of the wealthiest king, but probably that of all of Europe's nobility added together.[26] A substantial portion of this wealth flowed into the coffers of the religious orders, much of it in payments and endowments in return for liturgical services – Henry VII of England paid to have 10,000 masses said for his soul.[27] In addition to receiving many gifts of land, most orders reinvested wealth in buying or reclaiming more land, thus initiating an era of rapid growth which often resulted in extensive property holdings scattered over a large area. Although dwarfed by the huge monastic centre at Cluny, which may have had a thousand priories by the eleventh century, many monastic orders had established 50 or more outposts.[28] In the twelfth century, under the leadership of St Bernard of Clairvaux, the Cistercians protested against the extravagance of Cluny, but being wellorganized and frugal they quickly amassed some of the largest estates in Europe – many Cistercian houses farmed 100,000 acres and one in Hungary had fields totalling 250,000 acres.[29] In addition to gifts, much of this growth was achieved by incorporating previously untilled tracts as well as by clearing forests and draining submerged areas. For example, monks at the monastery of Les Dunes recovered about 25,000 acres of fertile fields from the marshes along the Flanders coast.[30]

This period of great expansion was motivated in part by population growth,[31] and in even greater part by increases in productivity. Until this era the estates were largely self-sufficient – they produced their own food, drink and fuel, they made their own cloth and tanned their own leather, they maintained a smithy and often even a pottery.

But with the great gains in productivity came *specialization* and *trade*. Some estates only produced wine, others grew only several grains, some only raised cattle or sheep – the Cistercians at Fossanova specialized in raising fine horses.[32] Meanwhile, the rapid increase in agricultural surpluses encouraged the founding and growth of towns and cities – indeed, many of the monastic centres themselves became cities. Writing about the great monastery of St Gall in Switzerland in 820, Christopher Dawson (1889–1970) noted that it was 'no longer the simple religious community envisaged by the old monastic rules, but a vast complex of buildings, churches, workshops, store-houses, offices, schools and alms-houses, housing a whole population of dependents, workers and servants like the temple cities of antiquity'.[33]

When estates grew into small cities and sustained many scattered outposts, and as they became specialized and dependent on trade, three very important developments occurred. First, they evolved a more sophisticated and far-seeing *management*. This was facilitated in the monastic estates by virtue of the fact that, unlike the nobility, their affairs were not subject to the vagaries of inherited leadership. The essential meritocracy built into the orders could ensure a succession of talented and dedicated administrators having the capacity to pursue plans of long duration. As Georges Duby put it, the new era forced monastic 'administrators to turn their attention to the domestic economy, to reckon up, to handle figures, to calculate profits and losses, to think about ways and means of expanding production'.[34]

Attendant to specialization was a second development, a shift from a barter to a *cash economy*. It simply was too complicated and unwieldy for a wine-making estate, say, to barter for its other needs, transporting goods hither and yon. It proved far more efficient to sell its wine for cash and then buy whatever was needed from the most convenient and economical sources. Beginning late in the ninth century, the reliance on cash spread rapidly. Perhaps the monks in Lucca (near Florence) were the first to adopt a cash economy, but it was well established across Europe when, in 1247, a Franciscan chronicler wrote of his order's estate in Burgundy that the monks

> do not sow or reap, nor do they store anything in barns, but they send wine to Paris, because they have a river right at hand that goes to Paris, and they sell for a good price, from which they get all their food and all of the clothes they wear.[35]

In contrast, although the estates of Greco-Roman times (as elsewhere in the world) were expected to produce rents in the form of agricultural surpluses for their rich landlords, they were entirely, or primarily, self-sufficient, subsistence operations. Moreover, they were so unproductive that a wealthy family required huge estates in order to live in style. But, even in its earliest stages, capitalism brought immense wealth to orders having only modest fields and flocks.

The third development was *credit*. Barter does not lend itself to credit – to conclude a trade by agreeing to a future payment of 300 chickens can easily be disputed as to the value of the owed poultry: are these to be old hens, roosters or pullets? But the precise meaning of owing someone two ounces of gold is not in doubt. Not only did the great Church estates begin to extend one another monetary credit; as they became increasingly rich they also began to *lend money at interest* and so did some bishops. During the eleventh and twelfth centuries Cluny lent large sums at interest to various Burgundian nobles,[36] while in 1071 the Bishop of Liège lent the incredible sum of 100 pounds of gold and 175 marks of silver to the Countess of Flanders and subsequently lent 1,300 marks of silver and 3 marks of gold to the Duke of Lower Lorraine. In 1044 the Bishop of Worms lent 20 pounds of gold and a large (unspecified) amount of silver to Emperor Henry III. There were many similar instances – according to surviving records, in this era bishops and monasteries were the usual source of loans to the nobility.[37] By the thirteenth century, monastic lending often took the form of a *mort-gage* (literally, 'dead pledge'), wherein the borrower pledged land as security and the lender collected all income from that land during the term of the loan and did not deduct this income from the amount owed. This practice often resulted in additions to the monastery's lands because the monks were not hesitant to foreclose.[38]

But the monks did more than invest in land or lend from their bursting treasuries. They began to leave their fields, vines and barns, and retire into liturgical 'work', conducting endless paid masses for souls in purgatory and for living benefactors who wished to improve their fates in the next world. Monks now enjoyed leisure and luxury. The monks at Cluny 'were given plentiful and choice foods. Their wardrobe was renewed annually. The manual labor prescribed by the rule [of St Benedict] was reduced to entirely symbolic tasks about the kitchen. The monks lived like lords.'[39] It was the same in the other great houses. And all of this was possible because the great monasteries began to utilize a *hired labour force*, who not only were more productive than the monks had been,[40] but also more productive than tenants required to provide periods of compulsory labour. Indeed, these tenants had long since been satisfying their labour obligations by money payments.[41] Thus, as 'religious capitalism' unfolded, monks still faithfully performed their duties, but aside from those engaged in liturgy, the rest now 'worked' as executives and foremen. In this way, the medieval monasteries came to resemble remarkably 'modern' firms – well administered and quick to adopt the latest technological advances.[42]

The virtues of work and frugality

Traditional societies celebrate consumption while holding work in contempt. This is true not only of the privileged elite, but even of those whose days are spent in toil. Notions such as the 'dignity' of labour or the idea that work is a virtuous activity were incomprehensible in ancient Rome or in any other pre-capitalist society. Rather, just as spending is the purpose of wealth, the preferred approach to work is to have someone else do it, and, failing that, to do as little as possible. In China the mandarins grew their fingernails as long as they could (even wearing silver sheaths to protect them from breaking), in order to make it evident that they did no labour. Consequently, capitalism seems to require and to encourage a remarkably different attitude towards work – to see it as intrinsically virtuous and also to recognize the virtue of restricting one's consumption. Of course, Max Weber identified this as the Protestant Ethic, so-called because he believed it to be absent from Catholic culture. But Weber was wrong.

Belief in the virtues of work and of simple living did accompany the rise of capitalism, but this was centuries before Martin Luther was born. Despite the fact that many, perhaps even most, monks and nuns were from the nobility and wealthiest families,[43] they honoured work not only in theological terms, but by actually doing it. In Randall Collins' words, they 'had the Protestant ethic without Protestantism'.[44]

The virtue of work was made evident in the sixth century by St Benedict, who wrote in his famous *Rule*: 'Idleness is the enemy of the soul. Therefore the brothers should have specified periods for manual labor as well as prayerful reading . . . When they live by the labor of their hands, as our fathers and the apostles did, then they are really monks.'[45] Or, as Walter Hilton, the English Augustinian, put it in the fourteenth century, 'By the discipline of the physical life we are enabled for spiritual effort.'[46] It is this commitment to manual labour that so distinguishes Christian asceticism from that found in the other great religious cultures, where piety is associated with rejection of the world and its activities. In contrast with Eastern holy men, for example, who specialize in meditation and live by charity, medieval Christian monastics lived by their own labour, sustaining highly productive estates. This not only prevented 'ascetic zeal from becoming petrified in world flight',[47] but sustained a healthy concern with economic affairs. Although the 'Protestant Ethic' thesis is wrong, it is entirely legitimate to link capitalism to a 'Christian Ethic'.

Thus it was that, beginning in about the ninth century, the growing monastic estates came to resemble well-organized and stable firms that pursued complex commercial activities within a relatively free market, investing in productive activities involving a hired workforce, guided by anticipated and actual returns. If this was not capitalism in all its glory, it was certainly close enough. Moreover, these economic activities of the great religious orders made Christian theologians think anew about their doctrines concerning profits and interest. Granted that Augustine had approved profits. But are there no moral limits to profit margins? As for usury, the Bible condemns it; but if interest is forbidden how can one buy on credit or borrow needed funds?

Capitalism and theological progress

Christian theology has never crystallized. If God intends that Scripture will be more adequately grasped as humans gain greater knowledge and experience, this warrants continuing reappraisal of doctrines and interpretations. And so it was.

Initial Christian opposition to interest and profits

During the twelfth and thirteenth centuries Catholic theologians, including Thomas Aquinas, declared that profits were morally legitimate and, while giving lip service to the long tradition of opposition to 'usury', these same theologians justified interest charges. In this way, the Catholic Church made its peace with early capitalism many centuries before there even were any Protestants.

Christianity inherited opposition to the charging of interest (usury) from the Jews. Deuteronomy 23.19–20 admonishes:

> You shall not charge interest on loans to another Israelite, interest on money, interest on provisions, interest on anything that is lent. On loans to a foreigner you may charge interest, but on loans to another Israelite you may not charge interest . . .

That interest could be charged of foreigners explains the role of Jews as money-lenders in Christian societies, a role sometimes imposed on them by Christians in need of funds. (It also had the consequence, usually ignored by historians, that medieval Christians with money to lend often masqueraded as Jews.)[48]

Of course, the prohibition in Deuteronomy did not necessarily bar Christians from charging interest since they were not Israelites. But the words of Jesus in Luke 6.34–35 were taken to prohibit interest: 'If you lend to those from whom you hope to receive, what credit is that to you? Even sinners lend to sinners, to receive as much again. But love your enemies, do good, and lend, expecting nothing in return.'

Charging interest on loans was thus defined as the 'sin of usury', and widely condemned in principle while pretty much ignored in actual practice. In fact, as already noted, by late in the ninth century some of the great religious houses ventured into banking and bishops were second only to the nobility in their reliance on borrowed money. In addition to borrowing from monastic orders, many bishops secured loans from private Italian banks that enjoyed the full approval of the Vatican. Hence, in 1229 when the Bishop of Limerick failed to fully repay a loan to a Roman bank, he was excommunicated by the pope until he had negotiated a new agreement under which he ended up repaying 50 per cent interest over the course of eight years.[49] The need for loans often was so great and so widespread that Italian banks opened branches all across the Continent. Although many bishops, monastic orders and even the Roman hierarchy ignored the ban on usury, opposition to interest lingered. As late as the Second Lateran Council in 1139, the Church 'declared the unrepentant usurer condemned by the Old and New Testaments alike and, therefore, unworthy of ecclesiastical consolations and Christian burial'.[50] Nevertheless, documents prove 'that in 1215 there were usurers at the Papal Court from which a needy prelate could obtain a loan'.[51]

As many of the great Christian monastic orders continued to maximize profits and to lend money at whatever rate of interest the market would bear, they were increasingly subjected to a barrage of condemnations from more traditional clergy who accused them of the sin of avarice. What was to be done?

Theology of the 'just price' and of legitimate interest

Obviously, people can't be expected to simply give away the products of their labour. But is there no limit to what they should charge? How can we be sure that an asking price is not sinfully high?

Writing in the thirteenth century, St Albertus Magnus proposed that the 'just price' is simply what 'goods are worth according to the estimation of the market at the time of sale'.[52] That is, a price is just if that's what uncoerced buyers are willing to pay. Adam Smith could not have found fault with this definition. Echoing his teacher, but using many more words, St Thomas Aquinas began his analysis of just prices by posing the question 'Whether a man may lawfully sell a thing for more than it is worth'.[53] He answered by first quoting Augustine that it is natural and lawful, for 'you wish to buy cheap, and sell dear'. Next, Aquinas excluded fraud from legitimate transactions. Finally, he recognized that worth is not really an objective value – 'the just price of things is not absolutely definite' – but is a function of the buyer's desire for the thing purchased and the seller's willingness or reluctance to sell, so long as the buyer was not misled, or under duress. To be just, a price had to be the same for all potential buyers at a given moment, thus barring price discrimination. Aquinas' respect for market forces is best revealed by his story about a merchant who brings grain to a country suffering a famine and who knows that other merchants soon will bring much more grain to this area. Is it sinful for him to sell at the prevailing, high market price, or should he inform the buyers that soon more grain will arrive, thus causing the price to decline? Aquinas concluded that this merchant can, in good conscience, keep quiet and sell at the current high price.

As to interest on loans, Aquinas was unusually confusing. In some writings he condemned all charging of interest as the sin of usury; in other passages he accepted that lenders deserve compensation, although he was fuzzy as to how much and why.[54] However, prompted by the realities of a rapidly expanding commercial economy, many of

Aquinas' contemporaries, especially the Canonists, were not so cautious, but began 'discovering' many exceptions wherein interest charges were not usurious.[55] For example, if a productive property such as an estate is given as security for a loan, the lender may take all of the production during the period of the loan and not deduct it from the amount owed.[56] Many other exclusions involved the 'costs' to the lender of not having the money available for other commercial opportunities such as buying goods for resale, or acquiring new fields. Since these alternative opportunities for profit are entirely licit, it is licit to compensate a lender for having to forgo them.[57] In this same spirit it was deemed proper to charge interest for goods bought on credit.[58] As for banks, aside from the exemptions noted above, they did not make straight loans at a fixed rate of interest since these would have been deemed usurious on grounds that there was no 'adventure of the principal'. The notion was that interest was legitimate only if the amount yielded was uncertain in advance, being subject to 'adventure'. But it took very little finesse for bankers to evade this prohibition by trading notes, bills of exchange or even currencies in ways that seemed adventuresome, but which in fact had entirely predictable returns and thus constituted loans and produced the equivalent of interest.[59] Thus, while the 'sin of usury' remained on the books, so to speak, 'usury' had become essentially an empty term.

Thus, by no later than the thirteenth century, the leading Christian theologians had fully debated the primary aspects of emerging capitalism – profits, property rights, credit, lending and the like. As Lester K. Little summed up: 'In each case they came up with generally favorable, approving views, in sharp contrast to the attitudes that had prevailed for six or seven centuries right up to the previous generation.'[60] Capitalism was fully and finally freed from all fetters of faith.[61]

It was a remarkable shift. These were, after all, theologians who had separated themselves from the world. Most of them had taken vows of poverty. Most of their predecessors had held merchants and commercial activities in contempt. Had asceticism truly prevailed in the religious orders, it seems most unlikely that Christian disdain for and opposition to commerce would have mellowed, let alone have been radically transformed. This theological revolution was the result of direct experience with worldly imperatives. For all their genuine acts of charity, monastic administrators were not about to give all their wealth to the poor or to sell their products at cost. It was the active participation of the great houses in free markets that caused monastic theologians to reconsider the morality of commerce, which was abetted by the marked worldliness of the Church hierarchy.

Unlike those in the religious orders, few holding higher Church positions had taken vows of poverty and many displayed a decided taste for profligate living. Bishops and cardinals were among the very best clients of 'usurers'. That is not surprising since nearly everyone holding an elite Church position had purchased his office as an investment, anticipating a substantial return from Church revenues. Indeed, men often were able to buy appointments as bishops or even cardinals without having held any prior Church positions, sometimes before they were ordained, or even baptized![62] This aspect of the medieval Church was an endless source of scandal and conflict, spawning many heretical mass sect movements, and culminating in the Reformation. But these worldly aspects of the Church paid serious dividends in the development of capitalism. The Church didn't stand in the way – rather it both justified and took an active role in the Commercial Revolution of the twelfth and thirteenth centuries.[63]

Italian city states

Although capitalism developed in the great monastic estates, it soon found a very receptive setting in the newly democratic Italian city states. In the tenth century they rapidly began to emerge as the banking and trading centres of Europe, exporting a stream of goods purchased from suppliers in northern Europe, especially in Flanders, Holland and England, their primary customers being Byzantium and the Islamic states, especially those along the coast of North Africa. Subsequently, the Italian city states industrialized and soon they were not only producing a large volume of manufactured goods for export across the Mediterranean, but they also began shipping a great many products back to northern Europe and the British Isles. For example, eyeglasses (not only for near-sightedness, but for far-sightedness as well) were mass produced by plants in both Florence and Venice and tens of thousands of pairs were exported annually.

Perhaps the most striking aspect of Italian capitalism was the rapid perfection of banking. The Italian bankers quickly developed and adopted double-entry bookkeeping. To facilitate long-distance trade, Italian banks invented bills of exchange, making it possible to transfer funds on paper rather than undertake the difficult and very dangerous practice of transporting coins or precious metal from a bank in Florence to one in Genoa, let alone from a trading company in Venice to a woollens dealer in England. Italian bankers also initiated insurance to guard against loss of long-distance shipments by land or sea. Perhaps the most important of all the Italian banking innovations was the perfection of modern arithmetic, based on the adoption of Hindu–Arabic numerals and the concept of zero. Even addition and subtraction were daunting chores for Romans, given their cumbersome numeral system. The new system was revolutionary in terms of its ease and accuracy, and arithmetic schools soon sprang up in all the leading northern Italian city states, eventually even enrolling students sent from northern Europe. With easy and accurate arithmetic available, business practices were transformed.[64] All of this accompanied the proliferation of banks in the Italian city states. By the thirteenth century there were 38 independent banks in Florence, 34 in Pisa, 27 in Genoa, 18 in Venice – a combined total of 173 in the leading Italian city states.[65] Moreover, most of these Italian banks had foreign branches. In 1231 there were 69 Italian banking houses operating branches in England and nearly as many in Ireland. In fact, until well into the fifteenth century every bank in western Europe was either in Italy or was a branch of an Italian bank.[66]

The proximate cause of the rise of Italian capitalism was freedom from the rapacious rulers who repressed and consumed economic progress in most of the world, including most of Europe. Although their political life often was turbulent, these city states were true republics able to sustain the freedom required by capitalism. Second, centuries of technological progress had laid the necessary foundations for the rise of capitalism, especially the agricultural surpluses needed to sustain cities and to permit specialization. In addition, Christian theology encouraged extremely optimistic views about the future which justified long-term investment strategies, and by this time theology also provided moral justifications for the business practices fundamental to capitalism.

And that's how capitalism arose in Western civilization. What Weber's famous thesis really represented was not research, but Protestant presumption. The arrogant claim that Protestantism freed Western civilization from the grip of a backward Catholic monolith not only prompted Weber (and probably explains why his thesis cannot be purged from the textbooks); it also spawned other presumptuous myths, several of which will be dispatched in Chapters 5 and 6.

5

The myth of the Protestant scientific 'revolution'

In 1676, Isaac Newton famously remarked, 'If I have seen further it is by standing on the shoulders of giants.' Unfortunately, too few who quote this line realize that not only was Newton quite serious, he was quite correct. Science did not suddenly erupt in a great intellectual revolution during Newton's time; this era of superb achievements was the culmination of centuries of sustained, normal scientific progress that began as early as the thirteenth century in Europe's newly invented universities. After all, Newton's First Law of Motion[1] was anticipated by Oxford's William of Ockham (1285–1349) with his insight that once a body is in motion, it will remain so unless some force, such as friction, acts upon it. This was further refined by the University of Paris professor Jean Buridan (1300–58) who developed the principle of *inertia* – that unless acted upon by an external force, bodies at rest will stay at rest and bodies in motion will stay in motion. Of course, Newton's First Law was merely the starting point for his magnificent system of physics, but, contrary to claims made on his behalf by the philosophers of the so-called 'Enlightenment', Newton didn't have to start from scratch. Rather, the glorious scientific breakthroughs of the sixteenth and seventeenth centuries were based on the work of a long line of natural philosopher 'giants'. Consequently, I prefer to identify this great era of scientific discovery as the 'coming of age' of

Western science rather than as a revolution, since there was no sudden break with the past.

Nevertheless, the notion that a scientific revolution erupted in the sixteenth century is so ingrained in our intellectual culture that Steven Shapin began his recent study with the charming line: 'There was no such thing as the Scientific Revolution, and this is a book about it.'[2] But, even if it proves to be impossible to lay this myth of revolution to rest, it must be possible to quash the second, far more troublesome myth: that the scientific revolution was accomplished by Protestants, Catholics lacking the necessary motivation and intellectual freedom. This myth is a close cousin of Weber's Protestant Ethic thesis and it too originated in the twentieth century. In what follows I will recount how this myth originated. Then, I will present conclusive evidence that it is false.

'Protestant' science

In 1936 Robert K. Merton (1910–2003) received his PhD in sociology from Harvard University where one of his major professors was Talcott Parsons (1902–79). Parsons was then a rising star who had earned his PhD in Germany and who had translated Max Weber's famous book on the Protestant Ethic into English. Merton also soon became an academic star, joining the faculty of Columbia University in 1941 and being awarded an endowed professorship there in 1947. Merton's early fame was based on his dissertation, which was published in full (all 272 printed pages) in the prestigious journal *Osiris* in 1938: 'Science, Technology and Society in Seventeenth-Century England'. In it, Merton attributed the scientific revolution to Englishmen who, as Puritans, were motivated by 'the Protestant ethic'.

After devoting many pages to showing that in seventeenth-century England more men took up scientific careers than ever before, Merton summed up his major argument thus:

> What we call the Protestant ethic was at once a direct expression of dominant values and an independent source of new motivation. It not only led men into particular paths of activity; it exerted a constant pressure for unswerving devotion to this activity. Its ascetic imperatives established a broad base for scientific inquiry, dignifying, exalting, consecrating such inquiry. If the scientist had hitherto found the search for truth its own reward, he now had further grounds for disinterested zeal in this pursuit. And society, once dubious of the merits of those who devoted themselves to the 'petty, insignificant details of boundless Nature,' largely relinquished its doubts.[3]

However, Merton did not really attribute the rise of science to the 'Protestant' ethic. Just as Weber really attributed the rise of capitalism to Calvinist Protestantism, immediately after the paragraph above, Merton shifted his discussion to 'the Puritan ethic'. As he put it: 'It was precisely Puritanism which built a new bridge between the transcendental and human action, thus supplying a motive force for the new science.'[4]

In support of this thesis, Merton sifted through the biographies of various English scientists to provide examples. He also gave some attention to the European continent where he confidently 'discovered' that 'even in the predominantly Catholic country of France, a large proportion of the scientific contributions were being made by Protestants'.[5]

Unfortunately, Merton paid little attention to the actual religiousness even of those English scientists he selected as examples. Most of them were not Puritans, but conventional Anglicans![6] In fact, Merton's definition of 'Puritan' was so broad that essentially no Christian could be excluded, not even Catholics.[7] As the distinguished Barbara J. Shapiro put it:

> Merton's nearly all-inclusive definition [of Puritanism] makes precise historical analysis nearly impossible because it fails to distinguish between the significant religious groups in seventeenth-century England. [Shapiro's footnote: His conclusions rest on a classification of the whole spectrum of Protestantism, with the exception of Lutheranism, as Puritan.] To hold that there is a close correlation between Puritanism and science, while including nearly the whole spectrum of English thought under the Puritan rubric, is simply to say that a correlation exists between Englishness and English science. This is true but not very helpful. If the object is to show the influence of Puritanism, viewed as a unique religious and social ethic, on science, it would seem necessary to arrive at a definition of Puritanism that reflects the actual historical division on religious questions in England.

In response to this problem, some have reinterpreted Merton's thesis to apply to Protestants, not just to Puritans. But that makes things even more absurd. How could one presume to test the claim that the Protestant Ethic gave rise to science, by only examining scientists in a Protestant nation? That could be proper if science has arisen only in England, but in that case no analysis of the religion of individual scientists would be necessary.

Moreover, even had Merton used an adequate definition of 'Puritan', his thesis still would suffer from his reliance on an unsystematic selection of examples. This flaw often vitiates historical studies, but it need not. Often it is possible to assemble data on an appropriate set of cases. And in this instance, I have done so.

First, I created a list of *all* the scientific 'stars' of the era beginning with the publication of Copernicus's

De revolutionibus in 1543 and including all born prior to 1680. In creating this list I ignored all aspects of the individual's biography, focusing only on his scientific achievements. I based my selections on study of the rosters provided in a number of specialized encyclopedias and biographical dictionaries, among which Isaac Asimov's *Encyclopedia of Science and Technology* (1982) was especially useful and reliable. I limited my selections to *active scientists*, thereby excluding some well-known intellectual figures of the day, such as Francis Bacon and Joseph Scaliger.

Having assembled a list, I then consulted various sources, including individual biographies, to determine the facts I wished to code for each case. In the end I had a data set consisting of 52 scientists – the complete list appears below arranged by nationality.[8] Opposite each name I have reported the individual's scientific discipline(s), religion, whether or not he had a university degree, whether or not he had served on a university faculty, and his social class origins: nobility, gentry, bourgeois or lower – these categories will be explained later.

English

Barrow, Isaac (1630–77)
Mathematics, Anglican
Protestant clergyman, degree, faculty, bourgeois.

Boyle, Robert (1627–91)
Chemistry/physics, Anglican
Protestant, degree, faculty, nobility.

Briggs, Henry (1561–1639)
Mathematics, Puritan
Protestant, degree, faculty, bourgeois.

Flamsteed, John (1646–1719)
Astronomy, Anglican Protestant clergyman, degree, not faculty, bourgeois.

Gellibrand, Henry (1597–1663)
Mathematics, Puritan Protestant clergyman, degree, faculty, bourgeois.

Gilbert, William (1540–1603)
Physics, Anglican Protestant, degree, faculty, bourgeois.

Grew, Nehemiah (1641–1712)
Biology, Anglican Protestant (his father was a Puritan clergyman, but he probably was a deist), degree, not faculty, bourgeois.

Halley, Edmund (1656–1742)
Astronomy, atheist, degree, not faculty, bourgeois.

Harvey, William (1578–1657)
Biology/physiology, Anglican Protestant, degree, not faculty, gentry.

Hooke, Robert (1635–1703)
Physics/chemistry, Anglican Protestant, degree, faculty, bourgeois.

Newton, Isaac (1642–1727)
Physics/mathematics, Anglican Protestant, degree, faculty, bourgeois.

Oughtred, William (1575–1660)
Mathematics, Anglican Protestant clergyman, degree, faculty, bourgeois.

Ray, John (1628–1705)
Biology, Anglican Protestant clergyman, degree, faculty, lower.

Wallis, John
(1616–1703)

Mathematics, Puritan
Protestant clergyman, degree,
faculty, bourgeois.

French

Descartes, René
(1596–1650)

Mathematics, Catholic, degree,
not faculty, gentry.

Fermat, Pierre
(1601–65)

Mathematics, Catholic, degree,
not faculty, gentry.

Gassendi, Pierre
(1592–1655)

Mathematics/physics, Catholic
priest, degree, faculty,
bourgeois.

Mariotte, Edme
(1620–84)

Physics, Catholic priest, degree,
not faculty, gentry.

Mersenne, Marin
(1588–1648)

Mathematics/physics, Catholic
priest, degree, faculty, lower.

Papin, Denis
(1647–1712)

Physics, Huguenot Protestant,
degree, not faculty, bourgeois.

Pascal, Blaise
(1623–62)

Mathematics/physics, Catholic,
degree, not faculty, gentry.

Picard, Jean
(1620–82)

Astronomy, Catholic priest,
degree, faculty, bourgeois.

Vieta, Franciscus
(1540–1603)

Mathematics, Catholic,[9]
degree, not faculty, gentry.

Italian

Borelli, Giovanni
(1608–79)

Biology/physiology, Catholic,
degree, faculty, lower.

Cassini, Giovanni
(1625–1712)

Astronomy, Catholic, no
degree, not faculty, lower.

Fabricius, Hieronymus (1537–1619) Anatomy, Catholic, degree, faculty, nobility.

Fallopius, Gabriel (1523–62) Anatomy, Catholic, degree, faculty, gentry.

Galilei, Galileo (1564–1642) Astronomy/physics, Catholic, degree, faculty, gentry.

Grimaldi, Francesco (1618–63) Mathematics/physics, Catholic priest, degree, faculty, gentry.

Malpighi, Marcello (1628–94) Biology/anatomy, Catholic, degree, faculty, gentry.

Redi, Francesco (1626–97) Biology, Catholic, degree, faculty, gentry.

Riccioli, Giovanni (1598–1671) Astronomy, Catholic priest, degree, faculty, unknown.

Torricelli, Evangelista (1606–47) Physics/mathematics, Catholic, degree, not faculty, lower.

Vesalius, Andreas (1514–64) Anatomy, Catholic, degree, faculty, gentry.

German

Bayer, Johann (1572–1625) Astronomy, Catholic, degree, not faculty, unknown.

Guericke, Otto von (1602–86) Physics, Protestant, degree, not faculty, nobility.

Kepler, Johannes (1571–1630) Mathematics/astronomy, Protestant, degree, faculty, gentry.

Kircher, Athanasius (1601–80) Biology/geology, Catholic priest, degree, faculty, bourgeois.

Leibniz, Gottfried (1646–1723) — Mathematics, Protestant deist, degree, not faculty, bourgeois.

Scheiner, Christoph (1575–1650) — Physics/astronomy, Catholic priest, degree, faculty, unknown.

Dutch

Glauber, Johann (1604–70) — Chemistry, born Catholic, no degree, not faculty, lower.

Graaf, Regnier de (1641–73) — Anatomy, Catholic, degree, not faculty, nobility.

Huygens, Christiaan (1629–95) — Astronomy/physics, Protestant, degree, not faculty, gentry.

Leeuwenhoek, Anton van (1632–1723) — Biology, Protestant, no degree, not faculty, lower.

Danish

Brahe, Tycho (1546–1601) — Astronomy, Protestant, degree, faculty, nobility.

Roemer, Olaus (1644–1710) — Astronomy, Protestant, degree, faculty, bourgeois.

Steno, Nicolaus (1638–86) — Anatomy, Catholic priest (convert), degree, faculty, gentry.

Flemish

Helmont, Jan Baptista van (1577–1644) — Chemistry, Catholic, degree, not faculty, gentry.

Stevin, Simon (1548–1620) — Mathematics/physics, Catholic, degree, not faculty, lower.

Polish

Copernicus, Nicolaus (1473–1543)	Astronomy, Catholic canon, degree, not faculty, gentry.
Hevelius, Johannes (1611–87)	Astronomy, Protestant, degree, not faculty, gentry.

Scottish

Napier, John (1550–1617)	Mathematics, Calvinist Protestant, no degree, not faculty, nobility.

Examination of the 14 English stars overwhelmingly refutes Merton: only three of them can be identified as Puritans: Briggs, Gellibrand and Wallis. Merton, and some others, have mistakenly identified Grew as a Puritan, but this is refuted by his book *Cosmologia Sacra or a Discourse on the Universe as it is the Creature and Kingdom of God*. There, in true deist fashion, Grew denied the possibility of miracles.[10] As for the other 11 English stars, 4 were Anglican clergymen, and Halley was an atheist.

Nor does Merton fare any better when we examine the data on France. Rather than 'a large proportion' of them being Protestants, there is only one Huguenot Protestant out of nine, rather overshadowed by the fact that four were Catholic priests! Moreover, one Huguenot is close to being proportional to the French population; Huguenots made up about 10 per cent of the population on the eve of the St Bartholomew's Day massacre in 1572.[11]

Given Merton's response to the devastating earlier rejections of his claim about Puritanism and English science, I doubt that even these data would have changed his mind. In 1984, Merton was given an unusual amount of space in the *American Journal of Sociology* to argue on behalf of his thesis that to reject it on the basis of the evidence against it would be to commit what he called the 'Fallacy of the Latest Word'. This 'fallacy' involves abandoning a theory 'as soon as it appears to have been empirically falsified'. He then asked, 'When are we to retain a hypothesis or theoretical conception in the face of facts that seem to refute it?'[12] In answer, Merton quoted Imre Lakatos that 'There is no falsification before the emergence of a better theory'.[13] Thus, Merton proposed that a false explanation of some phenomenon is better than none. How absurd. Oddly, Merton concluded his paper by calling, not for new theorizing, but for more research.

Of course, a much better theory had existed since before Merton: that there was no scientific revolution, only the culmination of normal scientific progress over several centuries and, moreover, that science arose only in Christian Europe because only medieval Europeans believed that science was *possible* and *desirable*. The basis of their belief was their image of God and his creation. This was dramatically asserted to a distinguished audience of scholars attending the 1925 Lowell Lectures at Harvard by the great English philosopher and mathematician Alfred North Whitehead (1861–1947), who explained that science developed in Europe because of the widespread 'faith in the possibility of science . . . derivative from medieval theology'.[14] This claim shocked not only his audience, but Western intellectuals in general when his lectures were published. How could this world-famous thinker, co-author with Bertrand Russell of the landmark *Principia Mathematica* (1910–13), not know that religion is the unrelenting enemy of science? In fact, Whitehead knew better!

Whitehead had recognized that Christian theology was essential for the rise of science, just as non-Christian theologies had stifled the scientific enterprise everywhere else. He explained that:

> the greatest contribution of medievalism to the formation of the scientific movement [was] the inexpungable belief . . . that there was a secret, a secret which can be unveiled. How has this conviction been so vividly implanted in the European mind? . . . It must come from the medieval insistence on the rationality of God, conceived as with the personal energy of Jehovah and with the rationality of a Greek philosopher. Every detail was supervised and ordered: the search into nature could only result in the vindication of faith in rationality.[15]

Whitehead was, of course, merely summarizing what so many of the great early scientists had said – René Descartes justified his search for the 'laws' of nature on grounds that such laws must exist because God is perfect and therefore 'acts in a manner as constant and immutable as possible'.[16] That is, the universe functions according to rational rules or laws. As that great medieval scholastic Nicole d'Oresme put it, God's creation 'is much like that of a man making a clock and letting it run and continue its own motion by itself'.[17] Furthermore, because God has given humans the power of reason it ought to be possible for us to discover the rules established by God.

Indeed, many of the early scientists felt morally obliged to pursue these secrets, just as Whitehead had noted. The great British philosopher concluded his remarks by noting that the images of God and creation found in the non-European faiths, especially those in Asia, are too impersonal or too irrational to have sustained science. Any particular natural 'occurrence might be due to the fiat of an irrational despot' god, or might be produced by 'some impersonal, inscrutable origin of things. There is not the same confidence as in the intelligible rationality of a personal being.'[18]

It should be noted that given their common roots, the Jewish conception of God is as suitable to sustaining science as is the Christian conception. But Jews were a small, scattered and often repressed minority in Europe during this era and took no part in the rise of science – albeit Jews have excelled as scientists since their emancipation in the nineteenth century.

In contrast, most religions outside the Judeo-Christian tradition do not posit a creation at all. The universe is said to be eternal, without beginning or purpose, and never having been created, it has no Creator. From this view, the universe is a supreme mystery, inconsistent, unpredictable, and (perhaps) arbitrary. For those holding this view, the only paths to wisdom are meditation or inspiration – there being nothing to reason about. But if the universe was created in accord with rational rules by a perfect, rational, Creator, then it ought to yield its secrets to reason and observation. Hence, the scientific truism that nature is a *book* meant to be read.

Of course, the Chinese 'would have scorned such an idea as being too naive for the subtlety and complexity of the universe as they intuited it',[19] as explained by the esteemed Oxford historian of Chinese technology, Joseph Needham (1900–95). As for the Greeks, many of them also regarded the universe as eternal and uncreated – Aristotle condemned the idea 'that the universe came into being at some point in time . . . as unthinkable'.[20] Indeed, none of the traditional Greek gods would have been capable of such a creation. But, worst of all, the Greeks insisted on turning the cosmos, and inanimate objects more generally, into living things. Consequently, they attributed many natural phenomena to *motives*, not to inanimate forces. Thus, according to Aristotle, heavenly bodies move in circles because of their affection for doing so, and objects fall to the ground 'because of their innate love for the centre of the world'.[21]

As for Islam, the orthodox conception of Allah is hostile to the scientific quest. There is no suggestion in the Qur'an that Allah set his creation in motion and then let it run. Rather, it is assumed that he often intrudes in the world and changes things as it pleases him. Thus, through the centuries many of the most influential Muslim scholars have held that all efforts to formulate natural laws are blasphemy in that they would seem to deny Allah's freedom to act. Thus did people's images of God and the universe deflect scientific efforts in China, ancient Greece, and Islam.[22]

It was only because Europeans believed in God as the Intelligent Designer of a rational universe that they pursued the secrets of creation. In the words of Johannes Kepler, 'The chief aim of all investigations of the external world should be to discover the rational order and harmony imposed on it by God and which he revealed to us in the language of mathematics'.[23] In similar fashion, in his last will and testament, the great chemist Robert Boyle (1627–91) wrote to the members of the Royal Society of London, wishing them continuing success in 'their laudable attempts to discover the true Nature of the Works of God'.[24]

Notice that Whitehead did not suggest that some kinds of Christians were more likely than others to pursue science. But it would not be inconsistent with his theory to suppose that Protestants might have been more likely than Catholics to become scientists. So, let us pursue that possibility with the data at hand.

Table 5.1   Religious affiliation of scientists

—	All	Continent only
Protestant	24	8
Catholic	28	28
Total	**52**	**36**

The claim that the 'Scientific Revolution' was the work of Protestants of any kind is clearly falsified by the data in Table 5.1. Only 24 of the 52 stars were Protestants, and with the English and one Scot removed, Catholics outnumbered Protestants by 28 to 8, which approximates the distribution of Protestants and Catholics on the Continent in this era. Indeed:

> there was nothing in the dogmas of Catholicism, Anglicanism, or Puritanism which made any one of them more or less favourable to science in general than any of the others . . . [in each, the majority held] that science should be welcomed as a faithful handmaid of theology.[25]

Escape from the university

Perhaps because Roger Bacon attacked universities as 'adverse to the progress of science', it has been conventional for modern historians of the rise of science to condemn the universities, especially since this provided additional grounds to attack religion.[26] As Richard S. Westfall (1924–96) put it:

> Not only were the universities of Europe not the foci of scientific activity, not only did science have to develop its own centers of activity independent of universities, but the universities were the principal centers of opposition for the new conceptions of nature which modern science constructed.[27]

This seems very surprising – at the very least it requires an account of how the universities turned against science and became bastions of the received wisdom, having previously sustained generations of distinguished scientific progress. No such accounts have been offered. That's because it never happened! The universities remained the primary institutional base for science in this glorious era just as they had throughout the prior centuries.

For example, what eventually became the celebrated Royal Society for Improving Natural Knowledge, later known simply as the Royal Society of London, began when a group of scientists started holding regular meetings at Oxford University in the 1640s.[28] The move to London coincided with the rise to prominence of Gresham College, located in London – a number of English scientists held joint appointments at Gresham and at Oxford and Cambridge.

In addition, 48 of the 52 stars (92 per cent) 'were university educated, not in the conventional sense of two or three years, but over an extended period [often] of ten years or more'.[29] Put in modern terms, these stars attended graduate school. For example, after four years at the University of Krakow, Copernicus went to Italy where he spent six more years at the universities of Bologna and Padua. Had he not been trained in Italy, it is inconceivable that Copernicus would have made any contributions to astronomy. Moreover, 28 of the stars served as professors for at least a period of their careers.

This is as it should have been because, rather than being opposed to science, the universities in this era were especially committed to it. As the distinguished historian of science Edward Grant put it: 'The medieval university laid far greater emphasis on science than does its modern counterpart.'[30]

Why England?

Many have claimed that England was the primary setting for this scientific era. Merton focused exclusively on England in pushing his Puritan explanation, and the prominence of non-academics among the London scientific set encouraged many to disdain the role of the universities. Although both of these interpretations are false, England was exceptionally productive of scientists – 14 of the set of 52 stars, many times more than would be expected on the basis of population. Why?

My explanation is that England led the way in science for the same reasons that it led the way in the Industrial Revolution[31] – its substantially greater political and economic liberty had produced a relatively open class system that enabled the emergence of an ambitious and creative upper middle class, sometimes called the *bourgeoisie*. While the rise of the bourgeoisie occurred all across western Europe, it did so earlier and to a far greater degree in England.

From earliest days the pursuit of knowledge has been the work of persons whose status was less than aristocratic. Aristotle tutored future kings, but he was the son of a physician. And the students at medieval universities 'were of a social position intermediate between the highest and the very lowest – sons of knights and yeomen, merchants, tradesmen or thrifty artisans'.[32] There were, of course, many universities educating these sons all across western Europe, but it was the case that in the seventeenth century more students enrolled in 'the English universities than at any time until the nineteenth century'.[33] In fact, beginning in the 1540s there was a remarkable explosion of education, at all levels, in England, resulting in a huge increase in literacy and a corresponding leap in the sale of books.[34] This was, of course, fully consistent with the Elizabethan court – 'commoners' such as John Hawkins and Francis Drake having played prominent roles in the queen's service.

Something else equally remarkable was taking place in England at this time as well: the lesser aristocracy were, in effect, joining the bourgeoisie from above. Unlike most nations in Europe (and elsewhere), in England only first sons inherited nobility. Hence, the first son of a duke succeeded his father as a duke. But his brothers were only known as 'lords', and their sons were without any title at all. As Lawrence Stone (1919–99) reported, '[these untitled heirs] were pouring into the universities and the Inns of Court'.[35] As a consequence of these developments, the segment of the population from which scientists were most apt to be drawn was much larger in England than on the Continent. Perhaps, for that reason, English scientific stars in the era were far more likely to have been of bourgeois origins than were continental scientists, as can be seen in Table 5.2.

Table 5.2   Class origins of scientists (percentage)

Class	England	Continent*
Nobility	7	13
Gentry	7	45
Bourgeois	79	16
Lower	7	18
Unknown	0	8
Total percentage	**100**	**100**
Total of scientists	**14**	**38**

* Includes the Scot John Napier.

These codes apply to each scientist's family. *Nobility* means one's father had a title. *Gentry* includes people of high social status, but no title, such as government officials, and large landowners, or, as Deirdre McCloskey put it, 'any dignified people just below the aristocracy'.[36] *Bourgeois* fathers were in business, or were members of the professions, clergy, professors and the like. *Lower* refers to those from peasant or labouring backgrounds, there being only eight among these stars.

As is obvious, the English scientific stars were overwhelmingly from the bourgeois, while more than half of the European stars were from the 'leisure class', gentry and the nobility – only 16 per cent were from the bourgeois.

This preponderance of bourgeois might seem to agree with those who have argued that the scientific enterprise was motivated by and sustained by concerns for practical advances in technology – especially in England.[37] The problem with this view is that at this time there were few if any technological applications made of the most significant scientific achievements. The lack of scientific applications was true not only of progress in physics and astronomy, but even in what might seem like more nearly applied sciences such as physiology. For example, it was several more centuries before Gabriel Fallopius' identification of the tubes leading from the ovary, named after him, was of any medical significance. On the other hand, this glorious era of scientific achievements also was marked by many new inventions and a great deal of technological progress. But the inventors and the scientists seem to have pretty much inhabited separate worlds. An example involves Denis Papin, one of the scientific stars, who claimed to have invented a better pump than the one designed by Thomas Savery and being widely used to drain British mines. To prove his point, Papin tried 'in vain to get the Royal Society to conduct comparative tests',[38] but the members did not find it a matter of interest. It seems not to have occurred to Papin to take his pump and demonstrate it to mine owners.

Rather than there being a direct linkage between innovations in science and technology, it seems more likely that both stemmed from and reflected the aggressive pursuit of progress by a rapidly growing, increasingly educated and achievement-oriented bourgeoisie. And, being by far the most bourgeois nation in the world at that time, that's why England played such a significant role in the rise of science.

In any event, the notion that the Reformations somehow prompted the rise of science is another myth.

6

The myth of Protestant individualism and suicide

It is a commonplace to identify Martin Luther as the 'father of individualism'. According to the Church historian Martin Marty, Luther was 'the greatest single agent in increasing the value of the individual'.[1] Or, to quote Derek Wilson, what Luther 'did, without realizing it, was to provide oxygen to human individualism'.[2] Of course, eventually Luther had no sympathy for individual freedom of religious choice, but 'his firm insistence on the priesthood of all believers, his call for people to read the Bible for themselves, and his rejection of authorities outside of the Bible and his own conscience all served to emphasize the value and the ability of the individual'.[3]

Max Weber certainly took this view, holding that the Protestant Ethic involved the economic isolation of the individual as it stressed the 'individual motives of rational acquisition by virtue of one's own ability and initiative'.[4] Weber also seems to have agreed with a long line of Western intellectuals that this may not have been a desirable development, as this emphasis on individualism 'had the psychological effect of freeing the acquisition of goods from the inhibitions of traditional ethics'.[5]

Alexis de Tocqueville (1805–59) was among the first to express deep regrets over the rise of individualism, which he traced back to the Protestant Reformation. Tocqueville is, of course, famous for his two-volume work *Democracy in America*, based on his perceptive nine-month tour of the nation in 1831. He had much praise for the young republic, but he feared it suffered from excessive individualism. Among his concerns was that individualism leads to selfishness and this can result in people not working for the common good, but for each to remain 'shut up in the solitude of his own heart'. Against this, Tocqueville urged that Americans spurn individualism and follow instead 'habits of the heart'.

A century later the distinguished French philosopher Jacques Maritain (1882–1972) expressed grave concern because the 'Reformation unbridled the human self'.[6] He quoted Luther: 'I do not admit that my doctrine can be judged by anyone, even by the angels. He who does not receive my doctrine cannot be saved.' Consequently, Maritain judged that 'Luther's doctrine is itself only a universalisation of his self, a projection of his self into the world of eternal truths . . . Lutheranism is not a system worked out by Luther, it is the overflow of Luther's individuality'. Worse yet, Maritain continued, 'Luther's case shows us precisely one of the problems against which modern man beats in vain. It is the problem of *individualism* and *personality* . . .'

And what is that problem?

> In the social order, the modern city sacrifices the person to the individual . . . and delivers the person, isolated, naked, with no social framework to support and protect it, to all the devouring powers which threaten the soul's life, to the pitiless actions and reactions of conflicting interests and appetites . . . To develop one's individuality is to live the egotistical life of the passions, to make oneself the centre of everything, and end finally by being the slave of a thousand passing goods which bring us wretched momentary joy.

Finally, Maritain returned to Luther: 'Luther's history . . . is a wonderful illustration of this doctrine. He did not free human personality, he led it astray. What he did was free the material individuality . . . the animal man.'[7]

Maritain's negative views of individualism were not unusual. In French, the word *individualisme* carries quite negative connotations. Indeed, the current Dictionary of the Académie Française defines the word as 'subordination of the general interest to the individual interest'.[8]

That negativity is not limited to the French, but is widespread on the political left. Thus, in 1985, Robert Bellah (1927–2013) and four co-authors took their title from Tocqueville when they published *Habits of the Heart: Individualism and Commitment in American Life*. These authors' antagonism towards individualism far exceeded Tocqueville's and perhaps even Maritain's:

> The central problem of our book concerns the American individualism that Tocqueville described . . . We are concerned that individualism has grown cancerous – that it may be destroying those social integuments that Tocqueville saw as moderating its more destructive potentialities, that it may be threatening the survival of freedom itself.

Presumably, that was why their book had five authors. In any event, they reported that their book was based on lengthy interviews with 'over 200 persons'.[9] One of these was a nurse they named Sheila Larson, who served as their prime example of the self-centred American. As the book climbed the bestseller list, Sheila soon enjoyed brief fame as liberal intellectuals around the nation joked about 'Sheila-ism', often connecting her to the Republicans. It turns out, however, as the authors subsequently revealed, there was no Sheila. The people who appeared in the book were all 'composite characters'. No individuals here.

In any event, Bellah and his co-authors could have cited many additional famous scholars as sharing their concerns about the 'evils' of individualism. Individualism has often been accused not only of fostering selfishness, but of leading to neurosis and despair – even to the point of suicide. Indeed, the claim that Protestant individualism is a major cause of suicide was the basis for an early sociological book that remains nearly as famous as Weber's *Protestant Ethic and the Spirit of Capitalism* – Émile Durkheim's *Le Suicide* (1897). As an introduction to Durkheim's book, it is useful to begin with why and how the French invented the field of sociology.

Discovering moral statistics

In 1825 the French Ministry of Justice began to collect criminal justice statistics from the prosecutor's office of each of the nation's departments, the geographical units into which France is divided, then numbering 86. Known as the *Compte general de l'administration de la justice criminelle en France* (General account of the administration of criminal justice in France), the *Compte* offered detailed statistics concerning criminal justice activities such as arrests and convictions. The data were submitted quarterly and published annually. The statistics were immensely detailed and broken down rather finely by age, sex, season and the like.

Once they had begun, the French soon expanded the scope of the *Compte* to include data on a variety of other things, including suicide, illegitimate births, military desertion, charitable contributions, literacy, and even per capita revenues raised by the royal lottery. These data soon became known as 'moral statistics' – so-called because of the moral implications of most of the actions being reported.

The first *Compte* was published in 1827 and copies were distributed to the nobility, members of parliament, and state functionaries.[10] Initially, the data were regarded as a somewhat interesting curiosity, but then they attracted the attention of a young attorney who quickly grasped their profound significance and devoted the remainder of his career to inventing empirical social research.

André-Michel Guerry (1802–66) was employed as a state prosecuting attorney by the Ministry of Justice in Paris when he received a copy of the *Compte*. As he studied the first *Compte* and then compared the moral statistics over a period of several years as new volumes appeared, Guerry observed two very profound patterns that people at the time found absolutely astonishing when he pointed them out in his masterpiece: *Essai sur la statistique morale de la France* (Essay on the moral statistics of France), published in 1833 by the French Royal Academy of Science.

The first of these patterns was that the rates were *extremely stable* from year to year. In any French city or department, every year almost exactly the *same number* of people committed suicide, stole, murdered their spouses or gave birth out of wedlock. And the *kinds of people* who did these things also was incredibly stable. For the five years from 1826 to 1830, the percentage of French women among those who were accused of thefts varied from 21 per cent to 22 per cent, and the percentage of persons aged 16 to 25 varied from 35 to 37 per cent.

Second, the rates at which these actions occurred *varied greatly* from one place to another. For example, the number of suicides per 100,000 population – calculated by Guerry as an average for the years 1827 to 1830 – varied from 34.7 in the Department of Seine (which includes Paris) down to fewer than 1 per 100,000 in Aveyron and Haute-Pyrenees. As for property crime, the data showed a rate of 73.1 per 100,000 in Seine in contrast with a rate of 4.9 in Creuse. Violent crime also varied immensely from department to department: 45.5 in Corse (the island of Corsica) down to 2.7 in Creuse and in Ardennes.

These patterns forced Guerry to reassess the primary causes of human behaviour. What could be more individualistic actions, more clearly motivated by private, personal, idiosyncratic motives, than committing suicide or murder? But, if these are indeed fundamentally individual acts, why didn't the rates fluctuate wildly from year to year? If individual motives alone are involved, how could it be that year after year the same number of people in Paris or in Marseille took their own lives or killed their spouses?

There was no alternative but to conclude that there are very powerful forces outside the individual that cause the incredible stability and the equally incredible variations from place to place that the *Compte* data revealed. As Guerry explained:

> If we were now to consider the infinite number of circumstances which might lead to the commission of a crime . . . we would find it difficult to conceive that, in the final analysis, their interplay should lead to such constant effects, that acts of free will should develop into a fixed pattern, varying within such narrow limits. We would be forced to recognize that the facts of the moral order, like those of the physical order, obey invariant laws, and that, in many respects, [these statistics] render this a virtual certainty.[11]

Then, by investigating whether social forces such as population density or the proportion of the population who were literate influenced variations on crime or suicide (they did), Guerry invented sociology, although it was another Frenchman, Auguste Comte (1798–1857), who coined the name in 1844.

The interest in moral statistics soon spread and before long most west European nations were collecting and publishing them annually. And as they appeared, these reports gave even more forceful proof of the immense variations from place to place. For example, the suicide rate for 1870 was 8.5 per 100,000 population in Sweden and only 4.0 in Italy. Why? Enter Émile Durkheim (1858–1917).

The curse of Protestant individualism

Durkheim did not face an intellectual vacuum when he first began to ponder variations in suicide rates. Twenty years earlier an Italian physician and professor at the University of Turin, Henry Morselli (1852–1929), had published a book based on suicide statistics. When he examined the suicide rates of seven German states (Mecklenburg, Saxony, Hanover, Bavaria, Wurttemberg, Nassau and Baden), Morselli noticed that the rate was higher for the Protestant states as a group than for the Catholic states. Since the science of statistics was yet to be achieved, Morselli was not sensitive to the perils of random variation and hence of the need to not base conclusions on so few cases. In the instance at hand, Saxony's suicide rate was far above that of the other six and greatly distorted the overall Protestant rate.

In any event, Morselli concluded that Protestants were more likely than Catholics to commit suicide and he explained it this way:

> Protestantism, denying all materialism in external worship and encouraging free inquiry into dogmas and creeds . . . tend[s] to develop reflective powers of the mind and to exaggerate the inner struggles of conscience. This exercise of the thinking organs, which, when they are weak by nature, is always damaging, renders them more sensible and susceptible to morbid impressions.[12]

When writing his book, also titled *Suicide*, Durkheim relied mainly on Morselli's statistics, with very little acknowledgement, and he also adopted Morselli's central observation and built upon his explanation, with no acknowledgement at all.

Durkheim began with the assertion that 'everywhere without exception, Protestants show far more suicides than do followers of other confessions'.[13] Then he formulated his 'theory' of why this is the case. Although Durkheim cited several causal factors, a fine analysis by Barclay Johnson demonstrated that they all were one: that Durkheim explained the Protestant propensity for suicide as a result of what he identified as *egoism*.[14]

As Durkheim defined it, egoism is a form of individualism – of putting one's self-interests first and thinking for oneself. Moreover, a group made up of individualists will be less strongly integrated by interpersonal bonds among its members, as each will tend to withhold some degree of commitment. Strongly integrated groups tend to protect their members from the worst intensities of life's ills, hence a lower suicide rate for Catholics and a higher one for Protestants. Durkheim put it this way:

> The only essential difference between Catholicism and Protestantism is that the second permits free inquiry to a far greater degree than the first . . . the Catholic accepts his faith ready-made, without scrutiny . . . The Protestant is far more the author of his faith. The Bible is put in his hands and no interpretation is imposed upon him [due to] this freedom of inquiry proclaimed by the founders of the Reformation . . . We thus reach our first conclusion, that the proclivity of Protestantism for suicide must relate to the spirit of free inquiry that animates this religion . . . [For] the greater concessions a confessional group makes to individual judgment, the less it dominates lives, the less its cohesion and vitality.[15]

For generations, social scientists assumed this to be the case, so much so that in 1967 Robert K. Merton credited the statement that Protestants are more likely than Catholics to commit suicide as being sociology's first, and thus far its only, scientific 'Law'.[16] But, as with the Protestant Ethic thesis and the claim that Protestants achieved the scientific revolution, it isn't so!

Durkheim was correct that groups having weak interpersonal bonds will have higher suicide rates, but Protestant groups are not less strongly bonded than are Catholic groups. Moreover, a series of studies, based on not only recent data, but also data for European nations dating from as long ago as 1870 – some of these being the very same data used by Durkheim – fail to show any Protestant effects on suicide.[17] Quite simply: Protestants do not have higher rates of suicide than do Catholics!

Durkheim may have made an honest mistake by failing to realize that Denmark's off-scale suicide rate in 1870 (25 per 100,000 population) greatly distorted the average rate for Protestant nations (with Denmark omitted, the average for Protestant nations was only 7.5, compared with 7.9 for Catholic nations). But one cannot overlook Durkheim's intentional misrepresentations as he tried to explain away the embarrassing fact that Catholic France had a suicide rate (15.0) more than twice as high as that of Protestant England (6.6) – the 1870 rate for Paris was 35.7, more than four times as high as London's rate of 8.6.

Durkheim's first attempt to dismiss the problem was to falsely claim that the English were a nation of uneducated illiterates: 'England, as we know, is the one Protestant country with the lowest suicides; it also resembles Catholic countries with respect to education. In 1865 there were still 23 percent of naval seamen who could not read and 27 percent unable to write.'[18] Since Durkheim knew that literacy was positively related to suicide, he must have meant this citation of English illiteracy to show that England had much less suicide than France because it had much less literacy. But he must have known that was not true since he was fully aware of published literacy statistics based on couples getting married, not on sailors, that showed that France and England were no different in terms of illiteracy!

Next, he tried to claim that England was not really a very Protestant nation. Rather, 'the Anglican church is far more powerfully integrated than other Protestant churches' despite the fact that 'England has been customarily regarded as the classic land of individual freedom . . . the Anglican clergy is the only Protestant clergy organized in a hierarchy. This external organization clearly shows an inner unity incompatible with pronounced religious individualism.'[19]

Durkheim knew better than this! And I will never understand how generations of sociologists who read this could have swallowed such an absurdity. All of the Lutheran state churches of Scandinavia were and are hierarchical. Anglicans were not even a majority of English churchgoers at the time Durkheim wrote.[20] Surely the presence of a multitude of nonconforming Protestant bodies in England and the many English conflicts, including civil war, over religious pluralism were not state secrets unknown on the Continent. Unfortunately, they seem to have been unknown to generations of sociologists.

On all counts, Durkheim's 'Law' required that England display one of the highest, not one of the lowest, suicide rates among European nations. Yet he could write:

> far from weakening our theory, the case of England verifies it. If Protestantism does not produce the same results on the continent, it is because religious society there [in England] is much more strongly constituted and to this extent resembles the Catholic church.[21]

But, even as Durkheim wrote that, he was surrounded by scholars who were equally certain that individualism had developed sooner and more fully in England than anywhere else on earth.

English individualism

Nearly every nineteenth-century scholar concerned to understand the rise of industrial capitalism in Europe, including Karl Marx, Max Weber, and a flock of historians such as Thomas Babington Macaulay, focused his attention on England because it was the earliest and best-documented example of the switch from the feudal to the capitalist 'mode of production'. As Marx explained, 'That is the reason why England is used as the chief illustration in the development of my ideas.'[22] In addition, England had the best, oldest statistics. All of these same scholars also believed that the crucial factor in this transformation was the rise of individualism, which they believed was reflected by the transition from being a peasant society.

What is a peasant society? It can be defined many ways, such as when most people live in rural areas and farm for a living. But that's not what Marx, Weber and the others had in mind. For them, peasant society referred to family structure. As Alan Macfarlane explained, in a peasant society the

basic element of society is not the individual, but the family, which acts as a unit of ownership, production and consumption. Parents and children are also co-owners and co-workers. The separation between the household and the economy which Weber thought to be a pre-requisite for the growth of capitalism has not occurred. For our purposes, the central feature is that ownership is not individualized. It was not the single individual who exclusively owned the productive resources, but rather the household.[23]

Hence, the challenge faced by those seeking to explain the rise of industrial capitalism was to explain why and how the collective peasant family structure had been transformed into the modern individual structure. To this end, Weber turned to Protestantism. In his view, Puritanism

> stood at the cradle of the modern economic man . . . [stressing the] individualistic motives of rational legal acquisition by virtue of one's own ability and initiative . . . [every Protestant] community was basically a confessional association of individual believers, not a ritual association of kinship groups . . . the great achievement of ethical religions, above all of the ethical and ascetic sects of Protestantism, was to shatter the fetters of the kinship group. These religions established the superior community of faith and a common ethical way of life in opposition to the community of blood, even to a large extent in opposition to the family.[24]

As Reinhard Bendix (1916–91) summed up Weber's view: 'the Puritan divines brought about a profound depersonalization of the family and neighborhood life' which was linked to a 'decline in kinship loyalties and a separation of business affairs from family affairs' which led to the 'isolation of the individual'.[25]

That became the settled opinion, repeated throughout most of the twentieth century. The illustrious David Riesman (1909–2002) took it for granted when he wrote his famous *The Lonely Crowd* (1950): modern individualism arose in the sixteenth century, propelled by the Reformation. Of course, Riesman thought individualism (inner-directedness) was a good thing, unlike Bellah and his many sympathizers.

But, good thing or bad thing, the Reformation had nothing to do with it! In 1978, Alan Macfarlane presented an avalanche of data showing that all of the measures of English individualism used by Marx, Weber, and the rest, predate the Reformation by centuries! He summed up his findings thus:

> In fact, within the recorded period covered by our documents, it is not possible to find a time when Englishmen did not stand alone. Symbolized and shaped by his ego-centric kinship system, he stood at the centre of his world. This means it is no longer possible to 'explain' the origins of English individualism in terms of . . . Protestantism. Individualism, however defined, predates sixteenth-century changes and can be said to shape them all.[26]

So, there it is. Martin Luther did not cause the rise of Western individualism. Neither is Protestant individualism a cause of suicide.

7

The myth of Protestant secularization

The prevailing wisdom has it that medieval Europeans inhabited an enchanted world, wherein religious places, images and activities were so ever-present that one could almost hear the angels sing. According to the celebrated Charles Taylor:

> religion was 'everywhere', was interwoven with everything else, and in no sense constituted a separate 'sphere' of its own . . . Atheism comes close to being inconceivable in [such] a world. It just seems so obvious that God is there, acting in the cosmos . . . acting as a bulwark against evil.[1]

Or, as William Manchester (1922–2004) put it in his best-seller *A World Lit Only by Fire*, 'there was no room in the medieval mind for doubt; the possibility of skepticism simply did not exist'.[2]

Then came Martin Luther, and the 'extravagant religious foliage of the late medieval world was radically reduced'[3] as he, and a long line of the Protestant divines,

> attempted to restrict the entire range of sacred persons, places, times and things . . . There were to be less sacred places and things: no more pilgrimages, relics, or sacred images. Even churches became more profane places . . . There were also fewer sacred times . . . so that there were far fewer moments in daily life when the sacred and its power were manifested in the world.[4]

As a result, the early Protestant theologians reduced religion from a surrounding experience to a *set of beliefs*. In so doing, they caused the 'disenchantment of the world', as Max Weber so famously put it.

Perhaps the most significant aspect of the world becoming disenchanted was 'a move from a society where belief in God is unchallenged and indeed, unproblematic, to one in which it is understood to be one option among others',[5] that belief in God came to be regarded as a *choice*. And, in the modern world, as some choose not to believe, the trend towards secularization accelerates.

In his monumental *Religion and the Decline of Magic* (1971), Keith Thomas traces the disenchantment of the world in marvellous detail. Of course, Thomas celebrated not only the emancipation of the people from magic and superstition, but also its presumed consequence: their embrace of secularity. Thomas put the case with unusual clarity and extraordinary detail, but he followed the now conventional narrative – that the Protestant desacralization of society caused the onset of secularization. Fortunately, not everyone agrees. Recently, Alexandra Walsham concluded her elegant summary by noting that 'the disenchantment thesis may have nearly run its course'.[6] And so it should have, as will be seen.

There is a second explanation of how Protestantism caused secularization that is entirely compatible with the first, and, if anything, even more widely embraced. By placing the burden on individuals to achieve their own salvation through the study of Scripture, licence was granted to endless organizational fragmentation and conflict. 'Once Pandora's Box of reform had been cracked open by Luther, there was little to prevent others from breaking with their church over their own understanding of the Bible. From here, there was no return. The modern world would grow increasingly pluralistic'.[7] And according to the prevalent view, the fragmentation of Protestantism into literally thousands of disputatious bodies has caused religion to lose its authority as each discredits the others. Hence, out of pluralism came secularization.

Most recently, this view has been expressed vividly and at very great length by the historian Brad S. Gregory, in *The Unintended Reformation: How a Religious Revolution Secularized Society* (2012). Gregory begins by admitting that '[l]ate medieval Christianity' suffered from a

> gulf . . . between its ideals and realities . . . Reformation leaders thought the root problem was doctrinal, and in seeking to fix it by turning to the Bible they unintentionally introduced multiple sorts of unwanted disagreement . . . Doctrinal controversy was literally endless, [and the conflicts] were destructive and inconclusive.

The response 'was to privatize religion and to distinguish it from public life'. The result was secularization, which in turn has 'led to the proliferation of secular and religious truth claims along with related practices that constitute contemporary hyperpluralism'. So, Gregory asks: 'What sort of public life or common culture is possible in societies whose members share ever fewer substantive beliefs, norms and values save for a nearly universal embrace of consumerist acquisitiveness?'[8]

The claim that pluralism led to secularization is not merely a historical thesis. In the hands of sociologists it became a general theory of social integration. Peter Berger put it best in his *The Sacred Canopy* (1969). Citing many 'founders' of the social sciences, Berger claimed that 'the classical task of religion' is to construct 'a common world within which all social life receives ultimate meaning binding on everybody'.[9] This can only occur where a single faith prevails, enabling it to spread a 'sacred canopy' – a universal religious perspective – over the entire society. Thus, Berger concluded that the rise of pluralism has doomed religion in modern societies and therefore an irreligious future awaits us all. As Berger told the *New York Times*, by 'the 21st century, religious believers are likely to be found only in small sects, huddled together to resist a worldwide secular culture . . . The predicament of the believer is increasingly like that of a Tibetan astrologer on a prolonged visit to an American university.'[10]

But they are all wrong. It is not merely that Protestantism did not cause secularization; nothing did! Let us start at the beginning.

Myths of medieval piety

Recall Chapter 1. Some enchanted world! The people in church: drunk, obstreperous, nasty, obscene or asleep. And these were the people who actually came to church in an era when very few did so. Nor was this true only in Germany. Keith Thomas combed the reports of English church courts and clerical diaries finding not only constant complaints that so few came to church, but that

> the conduct of many church-goers left so much to be desired as to turn the service into a travesty of what was intended . . . Members of the congregation jostled for pews, nudged their neighbors, hawked and spat, knitted, made coarse remarks, told jokes, fell asleep, and even let off guns . . . A Cambridgeshire man was charged with indecent behavior in church in 1598 after his 'most loathsome farting, striking, and scoffing speeches' had occasioned 'the great offense of the good and the great rejoicing of the bad.'[11]

As for atheism being 'inconceivable', and there being 'no room . . . for doubt', it should be noted that atheists frequently have been observed even in the most primitive societies.[12] As for medieval Europe, deism was well known and atheism was far from unknown, being frequently lamented by Elizabethan and Jacobean writers.[13] There clearly were groups of atheists among the aristocrats, such as the group around Sir Walter Raleigh, and there is evidence of atheists in humble circumstances too. This is well documented by Thomas, who concluded: 'Not enough justice has been done to the volume of apathy, heterodoxy and agnosticism which existed long before the onset of industrialism.'[14]

Granted that most medieval Europeans believed in the supernatural and resorted to magic when specific needs arose. But to attempt to compel or bribe various supernatural beings and forces to grant favours is a far cry from worship, and to equate this with living in an enchanted world is to embrace another myth.

None of this is 'new' knowledge. Most of the work I quote and cite above, and in Chapter 1, was written 40 or more years ago – Thomas' great volume appeared in 1971. Yet major scholars such as Charles Taylor still take the image of universal medieval piety so for granted that they don't bother to cite any support for it. This partly reflects the Balkanization of history – that scholars attend only to their special time and place. But, for the most part, it reflects that far too many scholars rely on the received wisdom, even on matters central to their subject.

The virtues of pluralism

Peter Berger was as wrong about the negative effects of pluralism as he was about the triumph of secularization. It is now well into the twenty-first century and religion was supposed to be all but gone by now. But, as we shall see, religion is stronger than ever worldwide.[15] And people don't seem to need a sacred canopy to shield them from religious diversity. Apparently they are sufficiently served by 'sacred umbrellas', to use Christian Smith's wonderful image.[16] As Smith explained, people don't need to agree with all their neighbours in order to sustain their religious convictions; they only need a set of like-minded friends – pluralism does not challenge the credibility of religions because groups can be entirely committed to their faith despite the presence of others committed to another religion. Thus, in a study of Catholic charismatics, Mary Jo Neitz found their full awareness of religious choices 'did not undermine their own beliefs. Rather they felt they had "tested" the belief system and had been convinced of its superiority.'[17] And in her study of secular Jewish women who converted to Orthodoxy, Lynn Davidman stressed how the 'pluralization and multiplicity of choices available in the contemporary United States can actually strengthen Jewish communities'.[18]

Given the American example, it should always have been obvious that the sacred canopy claims are silly. In the United States, in the most fully pluralistic nation that probably has ever existed, religion is thriving. And it is absolutely clear that it is competition among religious groups, each needing to effectively recruit members or fade away, that has produced these results.

In 1776, at the beginning of the American Revolution, despite the many Puritans and members of other intense religious sects who had settled there, only about 17 per cent of Americans were active in a local church – about the same as in Europe then (and now). As time passed and the number of denominations proliferated, membership rose. By 1850 a third of Americans belonged to a local church. By the start of the twentieth century, half of Americans belonged, and today about 70 per cent are affiliated with a local church.[19]

During the nineteenth century, the positive effects of American pluralism on religious participation were well known to European observers. As the German Karl T. Griesinger put it: 'Clergymen in America [are] like other businessmen; they must meet competition and build up a trade . . . Now it is clear . . . why attendance is more common here than anywhere else in the world.'[20]

The American experience of the Catholic Church is also quite instructive. Towards the middle of the nineteenth century, when a massive influx of Catholic immigrants began in America, they brought with them the low levels of participation and concern that prevailed in their European nations of origin. Initially, many of these Catholic immigrants defected to Protestant groups that aggressively missionized among them. But the American Catholic clergy quickly adjusted by adopting Protestant techniques (including revival meetings) and soon the American Catholic Church was far stronger and more effective than any national Catholic Church in Europe.[21]

Even in Europe, very modest variations in the extent of pluralism result in substantial differences in religiousness. The first application of the pluralism thesis to explain the low levels of religiousness in Europe[22] was limited to 14 major European nations[23] plus Australia, New Zealand, Canada and the United States. During the analysis, those European nations that were more than 80 per cent Catholic were omitted, but were dealt with later in a separate analysis.[24] The results were remarkably strong – pluralism accounts for more than 90 per cent of the total variation in church attendance across these nations. Moreover, the United States is not a deviant case, but lies close to the regression line – its unusually high level of church attendance being entirely consistent with its high level of pluralism. As for the Catholic nations, several studies have found that Catholic commitment is higher to the extent that Catholics are a minority of the population – that is, where they face greater competition.[25]

Then came three subtle and persuasive studies based on Swedish data by Eva M. Hamberg and Thorleif Pettersson.[26] Despite the very limited pluralism in Sweden, these scholars found very robust effects on church attendance. Even when pluralism consisted of nothing more than the extent of variation in the number and times of state church religious services, attendance rates responded quite significantly.

These studies establish that a major reason for Europe's low rates of church attendance is the stultifying effect of lazy, subsidized, monopoly churches who manage to minimize competition. They also demonstrate that the proliferation of Protestant denominations would not have resulted in secularization – even if secularization had been occurring.

The myth of secularization

Europeans have been predicting the death of religion for centuries. The first to specify a specific date was an Anglican clergyman, Thomas Woolston, who, writing in 1710, predicted that all traces of religion would have disappeared by 1900.[27] Fifty years later, Frederick the Great concluded that Woolston had been too pessimistic. Writing to his friend Voltaire, Frederick noted that 'the Englishman Woolston . . . could not calculate what has happened quite recently'. He concluded that religion 'is crumbling of itself, and its fall will be the more rapid'.[28] In response, Voltaire proposed that religion would be gone within the next 50 years – by about 1810.

And so it continued. Thomas Jefferson predicted in 1822 that 'there is not a young man now living in the United States who will not die a Unitarian'. Today, almost two centuries after Jefferson wrote, and subsequent to a merger with the Universalists, Unitarians in the United States number about 160,000 and in 2014 they put their Boston headquarters on the market because they were so short of funds.

Nonetheless, the same folks who still embrace the Protestant Ethic and who claim that Protestants produced the 'Scientific Revolution' continue to believe (and hope) that secularization is just around the corner – and with as little justification.

Consider these facts:

- All of the world's great faiths are growing, but Christianity is growing far faster than any of the others.
- Worldwide, 81 per cent claim to belong to an organized faith and many of the rest say they attend worship services.
- Regardless of their religion, 74 per cent of the earth's population say religion is an important part of their daily lives.
- Fifty per cent of the world's people say they have attended a place of worship in the past seven days.
- In very few nations do as many as 5 per cent say they are atheists; only in China, Vietnam and South Korea do atheists exceed 20 per cent; nowhere do they exceed 30 per cent.
- In every nook and cranny left by organized faiths, all manner of unchurched spirituality and mysticisms are booming. There are more occult practitioners in Russia than medical doctors.[29] Fifty-five per cent of Icelanders believe in the existence of *huldufolk* – elves, trolls, gnomes and fairies.[30] And nearly everyone in Japan is careful to have his or her new car blessed by a Shinto priest.

Where do statistics like these come from? The worldwide statistics come from the Gallup World Polls, which are annual nationwide surveys in 163 countries having 98 per cent of the world's population. I am grateful to the Gallup

Organization for giving me access to these extraordinary data. Other statistics, such as those on atheism, come from the World Values Surveys and from the International Social Survey Programme. These multinational surveys include far fewer nations than do the Gallup World Polls, but are freely available to anyone.

Of course, most of the secularization faithful are not troubled by the extremely high rates of Christian membership and participation in sub-Saharan Africa or the rapid rise of Christian membership in China. Although they expect religion eventually to disappear everywhere, most of them expect it to vanish first in the Christian nations and they point to the low levels of church attendance in Europe as proof positive. So, let us focus on Europe.

True enough, church attendance rates are lower in Europe than elsewhere in the world. But this can hardly be considered a substantial decline from medieval times! Moreover, few Europeans claim to be atheists, which is why the well-known British sociologist Grace Davie describes them as 'believing non-belongers'.[31] And, like Davie, many British scholars have seized upon this phenomenon to reject the secularization thesis entirely. As Oxford's David Nash put it in the subtitle of his recent article: 'Secularization's Failure as a Master Narrative'.

How has it failed? Because the definition of religion used to support the secularization thesis was too narrowly 'churchly' and failed to consider popular and unchurched forms of religious expression, counting them instead as irreligion.[32] Indeed, this point was made forcefully more than a century ago by Margaret Loane in her brilliant observations of working-class families:

> To count up churchgoers and chapel-goers and argue that the neighborhood is without religion or to estimate the

proportion of children and young persons in places of worship and then say 'religion has no hold on them' . . . is a serious error. It is a confusion of formal outward signs and inward spiritual graces. Many of the poor rarely attend church, not because they are irreligious but because they have long since received and absorbed the truths by which they live; while the idea that attendance at public worship is a duty does not occur to them and does not seem credible when suggested.[33]

As Loane noted, even towards the end of the nineteenth century, English churchmen and scholars were explaining a lack of church attendance as a result of a general decline in religiousness – soon to be identified as the secularization thesis. This especially appealed to the churchmen because it got them off the hook – if modernization was the cause, then they were not at fault (despite their lazy tenure). Thus, for nearly all of the twentieth century the thesis prevailed that if church attendance declines, that proves secularization is occurring even if there is no decline in, or there even is a corresponding increase in, non-churchly forms of spirituality. As Sarah Williams noted:

The simplistic identification of religion with institutional church practice [continued] . . . in much of the work done in the 1960s and 1970s . . . Today, few historians would commit the 'serious error' of confusing 'inward spiritual graces' with 'formal outward signs' in an unqualified manner. Most would nod in assent at Loane's emphasis and agree that the sum total of church- and chapel-goers is an inadequate gauge of religious fervour and even point to the importance of popular religion in the daily lives of working-class people.[34]

Thus far, this remarkable dismissal of the secularization thesis has been limited mainly to British historians who specialize in religion during the past several centuries. But the points they raise are equally valid when applied to the whole of Europe. And the truly pertinent question is: if people still are religious, why do they remain unchurched? Why are they content to be believing non-belongers?

Because lazy, obstructionist state churches do not effectively recruit them!

In most European nations there is nothing resembling a religious 'free' market. In many there are still established state churches supported by taxes. In most of the rest, a particular religion is the object of considerable government 'favouritism'. And in nearly all European nations, the government bureaucracy engages in overt and covert interference with all religious 'outsiders' and 'newcomers' that challenge the established religious order.

There are Lutheran state churches in Denmark, Finland, Iceland and Norway, while in Sweden, the established position of the Church of Sweden (Lutheran) was ended in 2006, although the government continues to collect a religious tax on its behalf. There are two state churches in Germany, the Evangelical Church (Protestant) and the Roman Catholic Church, both supported by taxes, and their clergy are classified as civil servants. Some cantons in Switzerland recognize Roman Catholicism as the state church; other cantons support an Evangelical Reformed state church. The Roman Catholic Church receives tax support in Austria and payments of more than 6 billion euros a year in Spain. In Italy, people choose the group to receive their church tax from a shortlist of Christian denominations and in Belgium there is no church tax, but the government provides very substantial support to Catholicism, Protestantism, Anglicanism, Judaism, Islam, and a category called 'nondenominational'. There is no church tax in the Netherlands, but the two primary Protestant churches and the Roman Catholics receive many large subsidies.

No religious group receives direct government support in France, but the Catholic schools receive huge subsidies and immense favouritism is shown to the Roman Catholic Church by the bureaucracy. Finally, the Church of England remains the established faith, but is not supported by taxes or government funds, being able to sustain itself from huge endowments built up during prior centuries of mandatory tithing.

These close links between Church and state have many consequences. First of all, they create lazy churches. The money continues to come whether or not people attend, so there is no need for clergy to exert themselves. Second, these links encourage people to view religion 'as a type of public utility'.[35] Individuals need do nothing to preserve the Church; the government will see to it. This attitude makes it difficult for non-subsidized faiths to compete – people will be reluctant to contribute to a church. Thus, when some German evangelists attempted television ministries, they drew viewers, but not contributions,[36] since religion is supposed to come free.

The existence of favoured churches also encourages government hindrance and harassment of other churches. The French government has officially designated 173 religious groups (most of them evangelical Protestants, including Baptists) as dangerous cults, imposing heavy tax burdens upon them and subjecting their members to official discrimination in such things as employment. Subsequently, Belgium has outdone the French, identifying 189 dangerous cults, including the Quakers, the YWCA (but not the YMCA), Hasidic Jews, Assemblies of God, the Amish, Buddhists and Seventh-day Adventists.

But even groups not condemned by parliamentary action are targets of government interference. As the distinguished British sociologist James Beckford noted, all across Europe government bureaucrats impose 'administrative sanctions . . . behind a curtain of official detachment'.[37] Many Protestant groups report waiting for years to obtain a building permit for a church, or even for a permit to allow an existing building to be used as a church. This is especially common in Scandinavian nations where it is often ruled that there is 'no need' for an additional church in some area, hence no permit is granted.[38] In Germany, many Pentecostal groups have been denied tax-free status unless they register with the government as secular groups such as sports clubs rather than as churches. Subsequently, the government sometimes revokes their tax-exempt status and imposes unpayable fines and back-tax demands on congregations.[39]

Nevertheless, many European scholars are adamant that their nations enjoy full religious liberty. To challenge that claim, it no longer is necessary to recite examples of state intrusions because Brian Grim and Roger Finke[40] have created quantitative measures of government interference in religious life. They based their coding on the highly respected annual *International Religious Freedom Report* produced by the United States Department of State. One of Grim and Finke's measures is the Government Regulation Index which reflects 'the restrictions placed on the practice, profession or selection of religion by the official laws, policies, or administrative actions of the state', scored from 0.0 (no restrictions) to 10.0 (only one religion allowed). On this measure, most European nations appear to offer a fair amount of religious freedom, although far less than the United States, France having the highest level of restrictions (3.9). But Grim and Finke's second measure, the Government Favoritism Index, tells a very different story.

The favouritism index is based on 'subsidies, privileges, support, or favorable sanctions provided by the state to a select religion or a small group of religions'. This index also varies from 0.0 (no favouritism) to 10.0 (extreme favouritism). Taiwan and Great Britain score 0.0 and Saudi Arabia and Iran each score 9.3. And while Afghanistan and the United Arab Emirates score 7.8, so do Iceland, Spain and Greece, while Belgium scores 7.5, slightly higher than Bangladesh's 7.3 and India's 7.0. Morocco scores 6.3, while Denmark scores 6.7, Finland 6.5, Austria 6.2, Switzerland 5.8, France 5.5, Italy 5.3 and Norway 5.2. Europe (but not Great Britain) has a religious 'market' highly distorted by government policies of favouritism, and that's that!

Fertility and faith

Under modern conditions, a fertility rate of 2.05 children per average female is required to keep the population from shrinking – one child to replace each parent and a tiny fraction to cover infant and childhood mortality. It is well known that European fertility rates are all far below the replacement level, even in Catholic nations such as Poland (1.39) and Italy (1.41). Were this to continue, eventually there would be no Europeans left in Europe. However, this would not result in a Muslim Europe since, quite unexpectedly, Muslim fertility has also dropped below replacement level (or is expected to do so in the next several years) in most nations, including those making up Europe.[41]

But there is a wild card in this deck. Religious Christian European women continue to have children well above the replacement fertility level. Table 7.1 was assembled by Tomas Frejka, of the Max Planck Institute in Germany, and Charles F. Westoff, of Princeton University.[42] They merged many samples in order to accumulate a very large number of cases. The results are definitive!

Table 7.1   Christian church attendance and fertility in Europe (women aged 35–44)

Women's church attendance	Fertility rate
More than weekly	2.74
Weekly	2.23
1–3 times a month	1.93
Less than once a month	1.83
Never	1.79

Source: Frejka and Westoff, 2008.

The implications of these fertility differences have been fully explored by Eric Kaufmann of the University of London in his book, *Shall the Religious Inherit the Earth?* (2010). Kaufmann noted that because only the irreligious sector of Europe's population is declining, while the religious sector is growing, only the irreligious European population is headed towards extinction, with the result that differential fertility may produce a huge religious revival in Europe.

Following up on Kaufmann, my calculations show that for Europe as a whole, the religious population will outnumber the irreligious population in about four more generations! The time span will differ from country to country depending on the current ratio of religious to irreligious, but the eventual outcome will be the same if everything else remains constant. Then, if the birth rate of religious Europeans is sustained at above the replacement level, the population will grow and the churches will be full – for the first time.

8

The myth of harmful Protestant effects on the Catholic Church

It is widely agreed that the Protestant Reformations had a positive effect on Catholicism by prompting the so-called Counter-Reformation, when the church fathers gathered at the Council of Trent in 1551–2, and again in 1562–3, wherein they achieved significant, beneficial reforms. That aside, the rise of Protestantism is assumed to have done and to continue to do the Church considerable harm, destroying its universality and often even forcing it to persist as a minority faith struggling to hold on to its members. That view is held by many Catholic prelates as well as by sociologists. Indeed, it was precisely because of such fears that the Church managed to shape government policies in Spain and the whole of Latin America, so that, until recent times, all Protestant competition was legally excluded.

Nevertheless, this too is a myth. The Catholic Church actually thrives on Protestant competition and is far more successful and effective when forced to confront it.

I begin with studies done in America, since the great geographic variations in Catholic strength, from being an overwhelming majority in some places to a tiny minority in others, serve as a fine natural laboratory.

Competition and Catholic commitment

The continental 48 United States include 171 Roman Catholic dioceses and these were the basis for a study of competition and Catholic commitment in 1996.[1] That year, 82 per cent of the people living in the Brownsville, Texas diocese were Roman Catholics. Next highest was Providence, Rhode Island at 64 per cent followed by Boston, Massachusetts at 53 per cent. In contrast, the diocese of Knoxville, Tennessee was only 2.1 per cent Catholic, and Jackson, Mississippi was only 2.2 per cent.

The study used four measures of religious commitment:

1 The *ordination* rate: the annual number of ordinations of diocesan priests per 100,000 Catholics (diocesan priests are always ordained in their diocese of origin). The extent to which young men are motivated to enter the priesthood reflects the overall level of rank-and-file commitment in a diocese.

2 The *seminarian* rate: the number of students enrolled in secular (as opposed to religious orders) seminaries. These are reported in terms of a student's home diocese even for students enrolled in a seminary maintained by another diocese.

3 The *priest* rate: the number of diocesan priests serving in the diocese per 10,000 Catholics. Because diocesan priests serve in their home dioceses, this is a measure of the history of ordinations in the diocese and thereby is less subject to momentary variations.

4 The *conversion* rate: the number of adult baptisms per 100,000 Catholics per year. Given the primary role played by the laity in bringing others into their churches, a high rate of conversions reflects a high level of enthusiasm among the rank and file.

It turned out that all four of these measures were very highly, negatively correlated with the percentage of Catholics in the dioceses. That is, the greater the extent to which Catholics were in the minority, the more highly committed they were. Put another way, in places such as Providence and Boston, where they are surrounded by co-religionists, Catholics tend to be complacent; in places such as Knoxville and Jackson, where they are a tiny minority in a sea of Protestants, Catholics are far more active and committed.

A second analysis was based on the 50 states. States are quite homogeneous in terms of per cent Catholic, and by using states it was possible to add two quite different measures of commitment:

1 The *Catholic Digest* rate: the number of copies of this national Catholic magazine sold in each state as a percentage of the Catholic population.

2 The *Marian apparitions* rate: in recent years there have been an increasing number of reported individual encounters with apparitions of the Virgin Mary, among Catholics worldwide.[2] This has given rise to an immense number of shrines and centres. Those located in the United States were transformed into state rates per 100,000 Catholics. South Carolina had the highest rate: 4 per 100,000. Massachusetts and New York had the lowest rates: 0.3 per 100,000.

These two measures of Catholic religiousness were very highly, negatively correlated with the per cent Catholic in a state, as were the four other measures. That is, where Catholics were fewer, more of them read the *Catholic Digest* and more of them had visions of Mary.

This is as it should be. People, including clergy, tend not to work harder than they must and this tendency aggregates into the well-known principle of elementary economics that monopolies tend to be lazy and inefficient. Moreover, this principle was applied to churches in the very first published work of modern economics. Writing in 1776 about established religions in general and the Church of England in particular, Adam Smith noted their lack of 'exertion' and 'zeal':

> the clergy, reposing themselves upon their benefices, had neglected to keep up the fervour of faith and devotion of the great body of the people; and having given themselves up to indolence, were incapable of making vigorous exertion in the defence even of their own establishment.[3]

Now for the really impressive example – how Protestants empowered the Catholic Church in Latin America.

Churching Latin America

Latin America was long regarded as the Roman Catholic continent, fully Christianized by missionary monks and Spanish swords by the end of the seventeenth century. Throughout most of the twentieth century, official church statistics reported that well over 90 per cent of Latin Americans were Roman Catholics. For example, the *National Catholic Almanac, 1949* reported that the per cent Catholic was 99.2 in Argentina, 98.0 in Bolivia, 97.0 in Brazil, 99.8 in Chile, and so on. These statistics were pure fiction. Ironically, they have been repeatedly used recently to 'prove' that there has been a massive defection from the Catholic Church in Latin America.[4] That too is pure fiction.

Although for several centuries the Roman Catholic Church was the only legal religion in Latin America, its popular support was neither wide nor deep.[5] Many huge rural areas were without churches or priests, a vacuum in which indigenous faiths persisted.[6] Even in the large cities with their splendid cathedrals, mass attendance was very low – as recently as the 1950s perhaps only 10 to, at most, 20 per cent of Latin Americans were active participants in the faith.[7] Reflective of the superficiality of Latin Catholicism, so few men entered the priesthood that all across the continent most of the priests had always been imported from abroad.[8] Meanwhile, the recent eruption of Protestantism (mostly of the Pentecostal variety) all across Latin America has enrolled millions of dedicated converts.[9] This challenge so upset the Catholic hierarchy that even Pope John Paul II, often a voice for religious tolerance, bitterly attacked the 'evangelical sects' as 'voracious wolves'.[10] But has the conversion of millions of Latin Americans to Protestantism really damaged the Catholic Church? One might well suppose that Protestant competition could invigorate the Catholic Church in Latin America. We shall see.

The lazy Latin monopoly

During the centuries of Spanish rule, the Catholic Church in Latin America was, for all practical purposes, a branch of government. Many government positions were staffed by priests and monks and the Church was lavishly supported by mandatory tithes collected on its behalf by the state. The Church also held huge land grants which yielded large agricultural profits. Hence, the Church 'had become the dominant economic force in colonial society by the end of the seventeenth century'.[11] By the end of the eighteenth century, in Peru 'there was scarcely an estate of any size that did not belong in whole or in part to clerics. In Lima, out of 2,806 houses, 1,135 belonged to religious communities, secular ecclesiastics, or pious endowments'.[12] In addition to its wealth, the Church was in complete charge of the educational system throughout Latin America. There were no public schools, only those provided by the church. And that's pretty much how things stood until the twentieth century.

Protestant missions

The first Protestants permitted to live in Latin America were small enclaves of foreign merchants, most of them British and Americans, but no Protestant churches or missionaries were permitted. Until well into the twentieth century there even were legal bans on the sale of Bibles in most nations of Latin America, which led to the widespread belief that only Protestants accepted the Bible.[13]

The Catholic legal hegemony began to break down late in the nineteenth century and early in the twentieth as 'liberal' revolutions strained the relations between the governments and the Catholic Church – the toleration of Protestantism being a form of political payback for the Church having supported the conservative regimes.[14] Initially, nothing much happened. Indeed, many prominent American denominations that were involved in substantial overseas mission efforts rejected Latin American ventures on grounds that these already were Christian nations.[15] But the evangelical denominations rejected this 'gentlemen's agreement' on grounds that 'the Catholic Church had failed to connect with the majority of the population'.[16] The result was a permanent split in American mission efforts, although little trace of the split now exists since the denominations that thought it improper to send missionaries to Latin America have pretty much abandoned all their missionary activities everywhere.[17] So it was that Latin America was missionized intensively, but only by conservative groups – with Pentecostal bodies soon surging ahead.

In 1996 there were nearly 12,000 American Protestant missionaries deployed in continental Latin America.[18] To put that total in perspective, there were substantially more full-time American missionaries in many Latin American nations than there were Roman Catholic diocesan priests! In Honduras there were five missionaries per priest, and missionaries outnumbered priests two to one in Panama and Guatemala. Even so, these statistics did not include thousands of American missionaries on shorter tours. But, more important, the number of American missionaries in Latin America has fallen dramatically since 1996. In 2004 there were only 5,116.[19] Why? Because they have been replaced by Latin Americans! In many Latin American nations today, native-born evangelical Protestant clergy far outnumber both foreign missionaries as well as local Catholic priests.[20]

The rapid increase in native-born Protestant clergy spurred the rapid growth of Protestant denominations in Latin America. But, although it is well known that this is taking place, statistics on actual Protestant membership have been scarce, scattered and of suspect validity. That is no longer the case. We now have data from the Gallup World Polls (described in Chapter 7) on the religious make-up of Latin America. Five tiny nations included in the Gallup World Polls were omitted on grounds that they are not an historic part of 'Latin' America. Four of them are former British colonies: Guyana, Belize, Jamaica, and Trinidad and Tobago. Haiti is French-speaking and never was part of Latin America. Puerto Rico was excluded because, being an American territory, it has had a very different history from the Latin nations, and Cuba was excluded because it lacks religious freedom. That leaves 18 nations that are culturally and historically identified with Latin America. I have combined the surveys conducted for all years from 2007[21] in order to maximize the accuracy of the statistics.

All respondents were asked their religious affiliation. The results are shown in Table 8.1.

Table 8.1   Protestants and Catholics in Latin America (percentages)

Country	Protestant	Roman Catholic	Other	Secular
Guatemala	41	55	1	3
Honduras	39	56	3	2
El Salvador	39	57	2	2
Nicaragua	34	59	4	3
Brazil	26	66	4	4
Dominican Republic	24	67	2	7
Costa Rica	23	71	4	2
Chile	20	69	4	7
Panama	17	78	5	
Bolivia	16	81	1	2
Peru	16	82	1	1
Colombia	12	85	2	1
Ecuador	12	86	1	1
Argentina	11	82	1	6
Uruguay	10	53	8	29
Paraguay	9	89	2	
Mexico	7	91	1	1
Venezuela	8	87	3	2

Source: Gallup World Polls.

These statistics reveal that Protestantism has become a major religious presence in most of Latin America. Protestants make up more than a third of the population in 4 of these 18 nations, and a fifth or more in 8 of them. The *Other* category includes indigenous and African faiths. The *Secular* category consists of those who said they had no religion. The high total for the *Secular* category in Uruguay (29 per cent) probably reflects the fact that more than 80 per cent of Uruguayans are of direct European descent.[22]

Unfortunately, it is impossible to separate the 'Protestants' into their constituent denominations. The major American evangelical groups such as the Assemblies of God, United Brethren, Churches of Christ, and various Baptist bodies are well represented. But there are many purely local Protestant groups as well, most of them having Pentecostal roots. For example, the Jotabeche Methodist Pentecostal Church in Chile probably has more than 100,000 members and its 'cathedral' in Santiago can seat 18,000.[23] In Brazil, an autonomous Pentecostal body known as Brasil Para o Cristo (Brazil for Christ) has attracted more than a million members.[24] In addition to large Latin-born Protestant groups such as these, there are hundreds of small independent groups.

Hence, the growth of Protestantism in Latin America has been the growth of meaningful pluralism. And the eventual result was that most Latin Catholic hierarchies responded very energetically. This has been ignored in nearly every published study of Protestant growth in Latin America. Thus Harvey Cox[25] enthusiastically repeated David Stoll's prediction, made in 1990, that five or six Latin nations would have Protestant majorities by 2010 and that Protestants would be on the verge of becoming majorities in several more nations. As it happened, that prediction was much too optimistic; only in four Latin countries do Protestants constitute even a third of the population. Of course, had the bishops continued to embrace their illusions and done nothing to compete with their Protestant challengers, Stoll's predictions might well have come to pass. And if observers failed initially to see that the Church would vigorously respond to the challenge, it was because the initial tactic endorsed by the bishops was primarily political rather than religious and was a resounding failure.

Liberationists

During the 1960s, as energetic Protestant groups began to make rapid inroads in Latin America, some Catholic theologians diagnosed their success as an appeal to the material deprivations of the masses. In response they fashioned a counterstroke that, although long on theological language and imagery, was essentially political. Known as Liberation Theology, it was a mixture of Marxism and Catholicism that aimed at 'mobilizing the poor for their own liberation'.[26] The proposed tactic to achieve this liberation was to unite small groups of lower-class Latin Americans into a form of utopian socialist commune, wherein they would have their political and moral awareness raised and serve as models of progress for others living in the surrounding area. These communes were called 'Base Communities' in accord with the long-range plan to rebuild societies from below, from a new base.

The primary theorist of Liberation Theology was the Peruvian Dominican priest Gustavo Gutiérrez who redefined salvation, discarding the emphasis on the individual and arguing instead that salvation is collective, taking the form of 'saving' the masses from bondage. Gutiérrez was a fully committed leftist who demanded 'a society in which the private ownership of the means of production is eliminated'. He often expressed his admiration for the murderous 'Che' Guevara, explicitly linked his theology to the work of Karl Marx, and not once did he criticize the Soviet Union. As Richard Rubenstein noted, 'Liberation theology is thus profoundly anti-American and deeply hostile to the bourgeois capitalist world. It manifests no comparable hostility to the communist world.'[27]

Liberation Theology greatly appealed to many American priests and nuns, especially those associated with the Maryknoll Mission Society, as well as to American and European intellectuals (especially social scientists) and to many clergy in Latin America – it was officially endorsed at a conference of the Latin American bishops at Medellin, Colombia in 1965. Although it was claimed that Liberation Theology was a response to the poverty of the masses, in reality national Catholic officials sanctioned Liberationists and their programmes to the extent that Protestant groups were making headway in their nations.[28] But to no avail.

Base Communities failed to arouse the masses to attempt to establish Christian Socialism. In fact, most of the Base Communities never developed beyond loosely organized, non-residential study groups that formed in urban neighbourhoods.[29] In keeping with the tepid sort of religiousness that prevailed in Liberation Theological circles, these Base Communities were not attractive to poor people, but appealed mainly to more educated, 'bookish' people.[30] Consequently, few Latin Americans ever became involved in Base Communities, probably no more than 2 million out of a total population of nearly 600 million.[31] It even has been suggested that Liberation Theology 'had more influence on Catholics . . . in Europe and the United States, than in Latin America'.[32]

Liberation Theology led nowhere because it was neither a revolutionary nor a religious movement, but involved a weak, self-cancelling mixture of each. More importantly, the attempt to offer religiously tinged 'solutions' to material deprivations did nothing to stem the rapidly rising tide of Pentecostalism, if for no other reason than, contrary to the consensus among social scientists (as well as bishops), compensation for material deprivations is *not* the basis of the Protestant appeal.

Materialist humbug

Social scientists interested in the rapid spread of Pentecostal Protestantism in Latin America have been in remarkable agreement about who is joining: the typical convert is a very poor, uneducated, married, older woman with health concerns, who lives in a rural area.[33] More is meant by these observations than mere description. They are interpreted to demonstrate that Protestantism, especially of the Pentecostal variety, appeals primarily to 'the damned of the earth'.[34] It should be noted that those I have cited above constitute an exceedingly distinguished set of scholars.

Unfortunately, most of the support for these generalizations does not come from survey data or even from personal observation of Protestant gatherings in Latin America. Instead, these claims often seem to have been assumed on the basis of social scientific preconceptions. 'Everyone' knows that religious movements are always 'the religious revolts of the poor'[35] that occur as 'the desires of the poor to improve the material conditions of their lives . . . become transfused with phantasies of a new paradise'.[36] Indeed, 'everyone' knows that participation in *any* social movement is prompted by material factors, rather than by idealism or faith. As Marx explained, to suggest that people act from religious motives is to attempt to explain a 'reality' by reference to an 'unreality' which is, of course, 'idealistic humbug'.

Even when scholars do not simply assume that material deprivations are producing Latin American Protestants, and rely instead on actual observations of persons attending services, they can be badly misled. Consider that *any* crowd of Latin Americans that is fully representative of the population will contain a very substantial percentage of poor, uneducated people. Hence, observing a preponderance of such people at a Pentecostal service wouldn't necessarily indicate anything except that Pentecostalism does not appeal exclusively to the rich.

Valid generalizations about the kinds of Latin Americans who convert to Protestantism require reliable surveys. And now that these finally have become available from the Gallup World Polls, they refute all of the material deprivation explanations.[37] It is not the poor who are joining – persons of all income levels are equally likely to join. Men are almost as likely as women to become Protestants and the unmarried are not different from the married. Young people are slightly more likely than those over 50 to convert. Those with health problems are not more apt to become Protestants, and rural and urban residents are equally likely to convert. So much, then, for deprivation theory. And so much too for Liberation Theology, since the growth of Protestantism in Latin America seems to be based on religious attractions. The best proof of this is the success of the second Catholic response to the Protestant challenge.

Catholic charismatics

What has come to be known as the Catholic Charismatic Renewal movement was initiated by an outbreak of 'baptisms in the Holy Spirit' that began at Duquesne University in Pittsburgh in 1967,[38] and was taken south by American priests in the early 1970s. It is revealing that they 'initially called themselves Pentecostal Catholics',[39] and aside from some distinctive elements of Catholic culture such as an emphasis on the Virgin Mary, it is difficult to tell Protestant and Catholic charismatics apart. Both conduct vibrant, emotion-packed worship services during which both clergy and members often engage in glossolalia, or speaking in tongues. Both put great stress on miraculous healing.

Having evolved into an international movement with a central headquarters in the Vatican, the Catholic Charismatic Renewal (CCR) now provides the backbone of Catholic commitment in Latin America. Although there are no reliable national statistics on CCR membership, it is estimated that there are at least 30 million members in Latin America. In any event, their impact on the religious life of Latin America has been immense. Just as Protestant Pentecostals fill soccer stadia for massive revivals, CCR revivals fill the same stadia. In addition, the CCR has established tens of thousands of weekly prayer groups which, unlike the Base Communities, have generated intense levels of public commitment. This was accomplished, not by sermons about how the Church could organize to mitigate material deprivations, but by sermons invoking the Holy Spirit, thereby activating religious motivations for religiousness.

Catholic renewal

Although there are no reliable statistics on CCR membership broken down by nations, other statistics indirectly reveal the energizing effect of the CCR. In 1960, in the whole of Latin America there were only 4,093 men enrolled in Catholic seminaries; by 2015 this had risen to 21,520.[40] Mass attendance has enjoyed a similarly huge increase, as can be seen in Table 8.2 overleaf, which shows the percentage of Catholics in each Latin American nation who said 'yes', when asked: *Have you attended a place of worship or religious service in the past seven days?*

Table 8.2   Current Catholic mass attendance in modern Latin America (percentage)

Country	Attended in past seven days
Guatemala	71
Colombia	68
El Salvador	67
Honduras	65
Ecuador	62
Costa Rica	62
Mexico	60
Paraguay	59
Bolivia	58
Nicaragua	58
Panama	57
Dominican Republic	53
Peru	52
Brazil	47
Venezuela	42
Chile	34
Argentina	31
Uruguay	20

Source: Gallup World Polls.

In most of Latin America today, Catholics are attending church at a truly remarkable level. In seven of these nations the weekly attendance rate is 60 per cent or higher – 71 per cent in Guatemala. Six more nations have mass attendance rates above 52 per cent. Compare this with Spain where only 31 per cent of Catholics say they attend mass weekly. Argentina and Chile have attendance rates about the same as Spain, and only in Uruguay (20 per cent) is attendance at the low level thought to have been typical of Latin nations several decades ago – and Uruguay is a deviant case in many other ways as well.

Table 8.3 shows the percentage of the Catholics in each nation who answered 'yes' when asked: *Is religion an important part of your daily life?* The level of subjective religiousness among Latin American Catholics is as astounding as their church attendance. Uruguay is much the lowest with only 53 per cent, but that is higher than in Spain (44 per cent).

Table 8.3 Percentage of Latin American Catholics who say religion is an important part of their daily lives

Country	Percentage
Paraguay	92
Honduras	91
Panama	90
El Salvador	89
Brazil	89
Bolivia	88
Colombia	88
Costa Rica	88
Dominican Republic	88
Guatemala	88
Nicaragua	85
Peru	85
Ecuador	83
Venezuela	75
Chile	74
Mexico	71
Argentina	67
Uruguay	53

Source: Gallup World Polls.

Of course, this is precisely the effect that pluralism should have had in Latin America unless the Catholic Church had failed to respond and simply faded away. That is, Catholic mass attendance should be higher where Protestants have been more successful, thereby creating greater pluralism.

There is a very high positive correlation between the per cent Protestant and Catholic attendance ($r = .451$ which is significant beyond the .05 level).[41] Where Protestants have been more successful, the Catholic response has been more energetic. A second test of the claim that pluralism has empowered Catholicism is that where Protestants have been more successful, Catholic subjective religiousness ought to be higher too. And it is ($r = .487$).

The Catholic Church has undergone a stunning awakening in Latin America. Where once the bishops were content with bogus claims about a Catholic continent and a reality of low levels of commitment, the Catholic churches in Latin America are now filled on Sundays with devoted members, many of them also active in charismatic groups that meet during the week. And the source of this remarkable change has been the rapid growth of intense Protestant faiths, thus creating a highly competitive pluralist environment. Contrary to the sociological orthodoxy, pluralism results in more active and effective churches.

That the Catholic Church finally thrives in Latin America could be considered as partly a gift from Martin Luther.

Conclusion
Prejudice and persistence

As is clear in Chapter 4, the myth of the Protestant Ethic and the rise of capitalism was convincingly refuted within a few years of its publication. And then, again and again – and yet again. But it won't die. It lives on in introductory sociology textbooks and among most sociologists who, not so long ago, ranked Weber's utterly debunked study as the fourth most important sociological work of the twentieth century. Why? Indeed, why do so many scholars continue to repeat nonsense about Catholic opposition to science and thereby attribute the scientific 'revolution' to Protestantism? The answer is as simple as it is distressing: the English-speaking world remains in the grip of the bitter anti-Catholicism that arose during the religious wars produced by the Reformations. And that prejudice acts to certify Protestant virtues.

Little has changed since Peter Viereck described 'Catholic-baiting' as 'the thinking man's anti-Semitism'.[1] Events that would have caused national outrage and been classified as 'hate crimes', had they been conducted in a synagogue or a mosque, or even in a Baptist church, have been downplayed and often excused by the media in the United States and Canada, such as when demonstrators interrupted a mass, screaming obscenities and throwing around condoms and used sanitary napkins, as happened in both Montreal and New York City. Granted that few academics in either the United Kingdom or North America would endorse these incidents, but most of them no doubt still agree with the New York drama critics and public intellectuals when they praised *The Deputy*, a play in which Pope Pius XII is depicted as having been complicit in the Holocaust. Indeed, academics continue to give favourable reviews to books making these same charges, despite the fact that an all-star group of Jews, including two prime ministers of Israel, condemned these claims and praised Pope Pius for his many effective efforts to save Jews during the Second World War.

Such behaviour inspired my colleague Philip Jenkins to write *The New Anti-Catholicism: The Last Acceptable Prejudice* (2003) – although a Distinguished Professor at Baylor, Jenkins is British and a member of the Church of England. As for scholarly anti-Catholicism, last year I published *Bearing False Witness: Debunking Centuries of Anti-Catholic History*. In response, several academics have accused me of being anti-Protestant, apparently unaware that I was raised a Lutheran. Worse yet, despite books such as Jenkins' and mine, anti-Catholicism will no doubt continue to thrive among English-speaking intellectuals – many of them routinely still refer to the 'Dark Ages' as an era of unmitigated backwardness imposed by Catholic opposition to learning and reason, although all qualified historians have long dismissed the Dark Ages as Protestant-inspired nonsense.

But we must keep at it. When I was a child, several women, who posed as ex-nuns, earned good livings by giving talks at American Protestant churches about the sexual escapades that went on in the convents between the nuns and their male confessors. No one any longer believes that. Maybe, in another generation, the Protestant Ethic thesis will be discarded as well.

In any event, despite all the myths and nonsense, I have no doubt that the Reformations were good for Christianity. Pluralism is what makes it the fastest-growing religion in the world.

Notes

Introduction: the mythical 'Protestant'

1 For a survey see Marshall, 2009.
2 Payton, 2010:224.
3 Instruction to Lutheran visitation inspectors, quoted in Strauss, 1978:252.
4 McGrath, 2007:7.

1 The myths of full pews, pious kings and limited monarchies

1 Walzer, 1965:4.
2 Murray, 1972: 92.
3 Coulton, 1938:189–90.
4 Farmer, 1991:336; Hay, 1977:64.
5 Niebuhr, 1929.
6 Cohn, 1961.
7 Quoted in Strauss, 1975:33.
8 Quoted in Hendrix, 2000:562.
9 Strauss, 1975:49.
10 Strauss, 1975:49.
11 Strauss, 1975:49.
12 Strauss, 1978:278.
13 Strauss, 1978:278–9.
14 Strauss, 1978:283.
15 Strauss, 1978:284.
16 Strauss, 1978:273.
17 Strauss, 1975:56–7.
18 Strauss, 1978:284.
19 Strauss, 1975:59.
20 Strauss, 1975:51.
21 Parker, 1992:45–6.

22 Quoted in Field, 2008:214.

23 Both quotes from Thomas, 1971:164.

24 Thomas, 1971:165.

25 Thomas, 1971:164.

26 Coulton, 1938:157.

27 Thomas, 1971:163.

28 Quoted in Thomas, 1971:163.

29 Obelkevich, 1976:279.

30 Strauss, 1978:211.

31 Dixon, 2012:116.

32 Dixon, 2012; Monod, 1999.

33 MacCulloch, 2004:324.

34 Chadwick, 1972; Duffy, 1992; Durant, 1957; Latourette, 1975; Ozment, 1975; Roberts, 1968; Tracy, 1999.

35 Chadwick, 1972:26.

36 Durant, 1957:639.

37 Bush, 1967; Hill, 1967.

38 Stark, 2004b: ch. 4.

39 Wuthnow, 1989:90.

40 Johnson, 1976:267; Woodward, 1974:19.

41 Inflation calculations in 'Dissolution of the Monasteries', Wikipedia.

42 Woodward, 1974:19.

43 Latourette, 1975:735.

44 Latourette, 1975:737.

45 Ozment, 1975.

46 Moeller, 1972; Ozment, 1975; Tracy, 1999.

47 Stark, 2004b:111.

48 'Relations between the Catholic Church and the state', Wikipedia.

49 Rubin, 2016.

50 Sorensen, 2016:94.

51 *City of God*, book 4, ch. 4.

52 Deane, 1973:423.

53 Excerpted in O'Donovan and O'Donovan, 1999:492.

54 *On Kingship*, book 1, ch. 6.

55 Hunter, 1965:16.

56 Sorensen, 2016:94.

57 Ekman, 1957.

2 The misfortune of state churches, forced piety and bigotry

1 Quoted in Grell, 1996:4.

2 Grell, 1996:5.

3 For example, Grell, 1995; Grell and Scribner, 1996; Heal and Grell, 2008; Hunter, 1965.

4 Zagorin, 2003:76.

5 Quoted in Zagorin, 2003:77.

6 Nelsen and Guth, 2015:69.

7 Baron, 1972:340.

8 Alwall, 2000:149.

9 Upton, 1990:100.

10 Jessup, 2010:170.

11 Pettersson, 1988.

12 Nelsen and Guth, 2015:99.

13 Ottosen, 1986:54.

14 Nelsen and Guth, 2015:99.

15 This material comes from Viola, 2015.

16 Gee and Hardy, 1896:458–67.

17 Field, 2008.

18 In Field, 2008:219.

19 In Field, 2008:217.

20 In Field, 2008:221.

21 In Field, 2008:220.

22 Nelsen and Guth, 2015:91.

23 Smith, [1776] 1981:789.

24 Duffy, 1987:88; Picton, 2015.

25 Alvarez, 2003.

26 Asberg, 1990:16–18.

27 Lodberg, 1989:7.

28 'Empty pews not the end of the world, says Church of England's newest bishop', *Daily Telegraph*, 9 June 2015.

29 North and Gwin, 2004.

30 Stark, 2016.

31 Stark, 2016: ch. 1.

32 Chazan, 1986:29.

33 Gritsch, 2012:xi.

34 Siemon-Netto, 1995.

35 Glock and Stark, 1966.

36 Shirer, 1960:236.

37 I have taken the excerpts of this work from the standard 55 volumes of *Luther's Works* published by Fortress Press. There is an unsourced edition of *The Jews and Their Lies* reprinted by Liberty Bell Publications and available on Amazon, but it appears to be incomplete and poorly translated.

38 Bainton, 1978; Brecht, 1985–93.

39 Kittleson, 1986:274.

40 Steigmann-Gall, 2003.

41 See 'Martin Luther and Anti-Semitism', Wikipedia.

42 Probst, 2012:30.

43 Probst, 2012:59.

44 See 'Martin Luther and Anti-Semitism', Wikipedia.

45 MacCulloch, 2004:666.

46 Probst, 2012:129.

47 Steigmann-Gall, 2000.

3 The misfortune of nationalistic states

1 Jones, 1987:106.

2 Stark, 2004b:56.

3 DeVries, 2010.

4 Bachrach and Bachrach, 2016:3.

5 Delbrück, 1982:327.

6 Oman, [1924] 1960:52.

7 Greengrass, 2014:xxvii.

8 Quoted in Michaud, 1855:51.

9 Porges, 1946:4.

10 De La Croix and Tansey, 1975:353.

11 Haskins, [1923] 2002:3.

12 Janin, 2008:73.
13 Nelsen and Guth, 2015:101.
14 Hayes, [1960] 2016:34.
15 Greengrass, 2014:xxvii.
16 Ozment, 1980:199.
17 Lindberg, 2010:35.
18 Sorensen, 2016:95.
19 Monter and Tedeschi, 1986.
20 Schulze, 1996:129.
21 Hutchinson and Smith, 1994:4; Hechter, 2000:5.
22 Schulze, 1996:121.
23 For a typically intelligent appreciation of nationalism see Himmelfarb, 1993.
24 'Conscription', Wikipedia.
25 'Conscription', Wikipedia.
26 For a study demonstrating that nationalism does lead to war, see Schrock-Jacobson, 2012.
27 Schulze, 1996:267.
28 Jünger, [1920] 1961:5.
29 Schulze, 1996:267.
30 Kistner, 1976:63.

4 The myth of the Protestant Ethic

1 Weber, [1904–5] 1992:39–40.
2 Weber, [1904–5] 1992:39.
3 Weber, [1904–5] 1992:65.
4 Weber, [1904–5] 1992:66.
5 Weber, [1904–5] 1992:67.
6 Weber, [1904–5] 1992:68.
7 Weber, [1904–5] 1992:71.
8 Weber, [1904–5] 1992:74.
9 Weber, [1904–5] 1992:104.
10 Weber, [1904–5] 1992:104.
11 Weber, [1904–5] 1992:116.
12 Ali, 1988; Eisenstadt, 1968; McClelland, 1961; Morishima, 1990; So, 1990.

13 Bellah, [1958] 2008.

14 Samuelsson, [1961] 1993:15.

15 Quoted in Delacroix, 1995:126.

16 Trevor-Roper, [1969] 2001:20–1.

17 Braudel, 1977:66–7.

18 Delacroix and Nielsen, 2001:545.

19 Sanderson, Abrutyn and Proctor, 2011.

20 Cantoni, 2015.

21 1 Timothy 6.10, RSV.

22 Little, 1978:38.

23 Collins, 1986:47.

24 Collins, 1986:55.

25 Collins, 1986:52.

26 Hayes, 1917; Herlihy, 1957; Ozment, 1975.

27 Dickens, 1991.

28 Little, 1978:62.

29 Johnson, 2003:144.

30 Gimpel, 1976:47.

31 Gilchrist, 1969; Russell, 1958, 1972.

32 Little, 1978:93.

33 Dawson, 1957:63.

34 Duby, 1974:218.

35 Little, 1978:65.

36 Little, 1978:65.

37 Fryde, 1963:441–3.

38 de Roover, 1946:9.

39 Duby, 1974:216.

40 Duby, 1974:91.

41 Duby, 1974:91.

42 Gimpel, 1976:47.

43 Dawson, 1957; Hickey, 1987; King, 1999; Mayr-Harting, 1993; Stark, 2003b.

44 Collins, 1986:54.

45 Chapter 48, The Daily Manual Labor.

46 Hilton, 1985:3.

47 Friedrich Prinz, as translated by Kaelber, 1998:66.

48 In Nelson, 1969:11; also Little, 1978:56–7.
49 Gilchrist, 1969:107.
50 Nelson, 1969:9.
51 Olsen, 1969:53.
52 In his *Commentary on the Sentences of Peter Lombard*, quoted in de Roover, 1958:422.
53 I have relied on the translations of Aquinas' *Summa Theologica* provided by Monroe, 1975.
54 Little, 1978:181.
55 Gilchrist, 1969; Little, 1978; Raftus, 1958.
56 Gilchrist, 1969:67.
57 Hunt and Murray, 1999:73.
58 Dempsey, 1943:155, 160.
59 de Roover, 1946:154.
60 Little, 1978:181.
61 Southern, 1970b:40.
62 For a summary see Stark 2003a.
63 Lopez, 1952:289; 1976.
64 Gies and Gies, 1969.
65 de Roover, 1963:75–6.
66 de Roover, 1963; Hunt, 1994; Lloyd, 1982.

5 The myth of the Protestant scientific 'revolution'

1 'Every body persists in its state of being at rest or of moving straight forward, except insofar as it is compelled to change its state by force impressed.' Newton, [1687] 1971:13.
2 Shapin, 1996:1.
3 Merton, 1938:439.
4 Merton, 1938:440.
5 Merton, 1938:479.
6 Kearney, 1964: especially 95.
7 Kearney, 1964; Rabb, 1965.
8 I have made slight revisions from the list and data reported in Stark, 2016.

9 Vieta was accused of being a Huguenot because he defended the rights of French Protestants. But he was always a Catholic, even having made a public statement of faith. See 'François Viète', Wikipedia.

10 Garret, 2011:4.

11 Hillerbrand, 2003: 'Huguenots'.

12 Merton, 1984:1108.

13 Merton, 1984:1109.

14 Whitehead, [1925] 1967:13.

15 Whitehead, [1925] 1967:12.

16 *Oeuvres*, book 8, ch. 61.

17 In Crosby, 1997:83.

18 Whitehead, [1925] 1967:13.

19 Needham, 1954:581.

20 Lindberg, 1992:54.

21 Jaki, 1986:105.

22 I have written extensively on this in Stark, 2004b: ch. 2.

23 In Bradley, 2001:160.

24 In Merton, 1938:447.

25 Kocher, 1953:4.

26 Gascoigne, 1990.

27 Westfall, 1971:105.

28 Gribbin, 2005:125.

29 Kearney, 1964:94.

30 Grant, 1984:68.

31 Stark, 2014.

32 Rashdall, [1936] 1977:III:408.

33 Kearney, 1964:100.

34 Stone, 1964.

35 Stone, 1972:75.

36 McCloskey, 2010:403.

37 Mason, 1950.

38 Landes, 1994:649.

6 The myth of Protestant individualism and suicide

1 Marty, 1993:53.

2 Wilson, 2008:344.

3 Sorensen, 2016:93.

4 Weber, [1904–5] 1992:122.

5 Weber, [1904–5] 1992:115.

6 Maritain, 1950:14.

7 Maritain, 1950:14–25.

8 Lukes, 1971:48.

9 Bellah et al., [1985] 1996:xliv.

10 Beirne, 1993.

11 Guerry, [1833] 2002:14.

12 Morselli, 1879:125–6.

13 Durkheim, [1897] 1951:154.

14 Johnson, 1965.

15 Durkheim, [1897] 1951:157–9.

16 Merton, 1967.

17 Pope, 1976; Pope and Danigelis, 1981; Stark and Bainbridge, 1996; Stark, Doyle and Rushing, 1983.

18 Durkheim, [1897] 1951:165.

19 Durkheim, [1897] 1951:160–1.

20 Currie et al., 1977.

21 Durkheim, [1897] 1951:161.

22 As quoted in Macfarlane, 1978b:37.

23 Macfarlane, 1978a:255–6.

24 As quoted in Macfarlane, 1978b:50.

25 Bendix, 1966:70–1.

26 Macfarlane, 1978b:50.

7 The myth of Protestant secularization

1 Taylor, 2007:2, 26.

2 Manchester, 1993:20.

3 Headley, 1987:21.

4 R. W. Scribner, MS quoted in Headley, 1987:28.

5 Taylor, 2007:3.

6 Walsham, 2008:528.

7 Sorensen, 2016:94.

8 Gregory, 2012:21.

9 Berger, 1969:133–4.

10 Berger, 1968.

11 Thomas, 1971:161–2.

12 Geertz, 1966.

13 Thomas, 1971:166.

14 Thomas, 1971:173.

15 Stark, 2015.

16 Smith, 1998:106.

17 Neitz, 1987:257–8.

18 Davidman, 1991:204.

19 Finke and Stark, 1992; Stark, 2008.

20 Grund in Powell (ed.), 1967:77,80.

21 Finke and Stark, 1992.

22 Iannaccone, 1991.

23 Austria, Belgium, Denmark, Finland, France, Great Britain, Germany (West), Ireland, Italy, Netherlands, Norway, Spain, Sweden, Switzerland.

24 Stark, 1992, 1998.

25 Stark, 1992, 1998.

26 Hamberg and Pettersson, 1994, 1997; Pettersson and Hamberg, 1997.

27 Woolston, 1735.

28 Quoted in Redman, 1949:26.

29 Stark, 2015:50.

30 Tomasson, 1980.

31 Davie, 1994.

32 For a brilliant summary see Clark, 2012.

33 Loane, [1906] 2012:26. Brought to my attention by Williams, 1999:1.

34 Williams, 1999:2–3.

35 Berger, Davie and Fokas, 2008:16.

36 Schmied, 1996.

37 Beckford, 1985:286.

38 Lodberg, 1989.

39 Selthoffer, 1997.

40 Grim and Finke, 2006.

41 Eberstadt and Shah, 2012.
42 Frejka and Westoff, 2008.

8 The myth of harmful Protestant effects on the Catholic Church

1 Stark, 1998.
2 Zimdars-Swartz, 1991.
3 Smith, [1776] 1981:789.
4 Encarnatión, 2013.
5 Stark, 1992.
6 Robinson, 1923.
7 Chesnut, 2003b:61; Gill, 1998:68; Martin, 1990:57–8.
8 Gill, 1998:86.
9 Chesnut, 1997, 2003a, 2003b; Gill, 1998; Freston, 2008; Martin, 1990; Stoll, 1990.
10 *Miami Herald*, 16 October 1992.
11 Chesnut, 2003a:22.
12 Mecham, [1934] 1966:38.
13 Klaiber, 1970; Montgomery, 1979.
14 Gill, 1998.
15 Nuñez and Taylor, 1989.
16 Gill, 1998:82.
17 Stark and Finke, 2000:153, Table 8.
18 Siewert and Valdez, 1997.
19 Welliver and Northcutt, 2004:32.
20 Stoll, 1990:6.
21 Prior to 2007, the Gallup World Poll did not distinguish Protestants and Catholics, but classified both as 'Christians'.
22 Barrett, Kurian and Johnson, 2001.
23 Jenkins, 2002:64; Martin, 1990, 143.
24 Jenkins, 2002:64.
25 Cox, 1995:168.
26 Drogus, 1995:465.
27 Rubenstein, 1985–6:162.
28 Gill, 1998.
29 Gooren, 2002.

30 Burdick, 1993; Hewitt, 1991; Mariz, 1994.

31 Cavendish, 1994; Hewitt, 1991.

32 Gooren, 2002:30.

33 Brusco, 1993, 1995; Burdick, 1993; Chesnut, 2003a,b, 1997; Cox, 1995; Gill, 1998; Martin, 1990, 2002; Stoll, 1993, 1990.

34 Martin, 2002:3.

35 Niebuhr, 1929:19.

36 Cohn, 1961:xiii.

37 The results are reported in detail in Stark and Smith, 2010.

38 Laurentin, 1977; Mansfield, 1992.

39 Chesnut, 2003a:61.

40 *Catholic Almanac*, 1961, 2016.

41 For all correlations reported in this study, a scatterplot was examined and statistical tests performed to guard against an outlying case(s) distorting the results.

Conclusion: prejudice and persistence

1 Viereck, 1953:45.

Bibliography

Ali, Abba. 1988. 'Scaling an Islamic Work Ethic'. *Journal of Social Psychology* 128:575–83.

Alvarez, Lizette. 2003. 'Tarback Journal: Fury, God, and the Pastor's Disbelief'. *New York Times*, World Section, 8 July.

Alwall, Jonas. 2000. 'Religious Liberty in Sweden: An Overview'. *Journal of Church and State* 42:147–71.

Asberg, Christer. 1990. 'The Swedish Bible Commission and Project NT 81'. In Gunnar Hanson (ed.), *Bible Reading in Sweden*, 15–22. Uppsala: University of Uppsala Press.

Bachrach, Bernard S. and David S. Bachrach. 2016. *Warfare in Medieval Europe c.400–1453*. New York: Routledge.

Bainton, Roland. 1978. *Here I Stand: A Life of Martin Luther*. Nashville, TN: Abingdon Press.

Baron, Salo Wittmayer. 1972. *Ancient and Medieval Jewish History*. New Brunswick, NJ: Rutgers University Press.

Barrett, David B., George T. Kurian and Todd M. Johnson. 2001. *World Christian Encyclopedia*, 2nd edn. Oxford: Oxford University Press.

Beckford, James A. 1985. *Cult Controversies: The Societal Response to New Religions*. London: Tavistock Publications.

Beirne, Piers. 1993. *Inventing Criminology*. Albany, NY: State University of New York Press.

Bellah, Robert N. [1958] 2008. *Tokugawa Religion*. New York: Simon & Schuster.

Bellah, Robert N., Richard Madsen, William M. Sullivan, Ann Swidler and Steven M. Tipton. [1985] 1996. *Habits of the Heart*. Berkeley, CA: University of California Press.

Bendix, Reinhard. 1966. *Max Weber: An Intellectual Portrait*. New York: Doubleday.

Berger, Peter. 1968. 'A Bleak Outlook Seen for Religion'. *New York Times*, 25 April, 3.

Bibliography

Berger, Peter. 1969. *The Sacred Canopy*. New York: Doubleday Anchor Books.

Berger, Peter. 2014. *The Many Altars of Modernity: Toward a Paradigm for Religion in a Pluralist Age*. Boston, MA: Walter de Gruyter.

Berger, Peter, Grace Davie and Effie Fokas. 2008. *Religious America, Secular Europe?* Burlington, VT: Ashgate.

Bradley, Walter I. 2001. 'The "Just So" Universe: The Fine-Tuning of Constants and Conditions in the Cosmos'. In William A. Demski and James M. Kushiner (eds), *Signs of Intelligence: Understanding Intelligent Design*, 157–70. Grand Rapids, MI: Brazos Press.

Braudel, Fernand. 1977. *Afterthoughts on Material Civilization and Capitalism*. Baltimore, MD: Johns Hopkins University Press.

Brecht, Martin. 1985–93. *Martin Luther*, 3 vols. Minneapolis, MN: Fortress Press.

Brusco, Elizabeth. 1993. 'The Reformation of Machismo'. In Virginia Garrard-Burnett and David Stoll (eds), *Rethinking Protestantism in Latin America*, 143–58. Philadelphia, PA: Temple University Press.

Brusco, Elizabeth. 1995. *The Reformation of Machismo: Evangelical Conversion and Gender in Columbia*. Austin, TX: University of Texas Press.

Burdick, John. 1993. *Looking for God in Brazil*. Berkeley, CA: University of California Press.

Bush, M. L. 1967. *Renaissance, Reformation, and the Outer World, 1450–1660*. London: Blandford.

Calleo, David P. 2003. *Rethinking Europe's Future*. Princeton, NJ: Princeton University Press.

Cantoni, Davide. 2015. 'The Economic Effects of the Protestant Reformation: Testing the Weber Hypothesis in the German Lands'. *Journal of the European Economic Association* 13:561–98.

Cavendish, James C. 1994. 'Christian Base Communities and the Building of Democracy: Brazil and Chile'. *Sociology of Religion* 55:179–95.

Chadwick, Owen. 1972. *The Reformation*, rev. edn. London: Penguin.

Chazan, Robert. 1986. *European Jewry and the First Crusade.* Berkeley, CA: University of California Press.

Chesnut, R. Andrew. 1997. *Born Again in Brazil.* New Brunswick, NJ: Rutgers University Press.

Chesnut, R. Andrew. 2003a. *Competitive Spirits: Latin America's New Religious Economy.* Oxford: Oxford University Press.

Chesnut, R. Andrew. 2003b. 'A Preferential Option for the Spirit: The Catholic Charismatic Renewal in Latin America's New Religious Economy'. *Latin American Politics and Society* 45:55–85.

Clark, J. C. D. 2012. 'Secularization and Modernization: The Failure of the "Grand Narrative"'. *Historical Journal* 55:161–94.

Cohn, Norman. 1961. *The Pursuit of the Millennium,* 2nd edn. New York: Harper Torchbooks.

Collins, Randall. 1986. *Weberian Sociological Theory.* Cambridge: Cambridge University Press.

Coulton, G. G. 1938. *Medieval Panorama.* New York: Macmillan.

Cox, Harvey. 1995. *Fire from Heaven: The Rise of Pentecostal Spirituality and the Reshaping of Religion in the Twenty-First Century.* Cambridge, MA: Da Capo Press.

Crosby, Alfred W. 1997. *The Measure of Reality.* Cambridge: Cambridge University Press.

Currie, Robert, Alan Gilbert and Lee Horsley. 1977. *Churches and Churchgoers.* Oxford: Oxford University Press.

Davidman, Lynn. 1991. *Tradition in a Rootless World: Women Turn to Orthodox Judaism.* Berkeley, CA: University of California Press.

Davie, Grace. 1994. *Religion in Britain since 1945: Believing without Belonging.* Oxford: Blackwell.

Dawson, J. M. 1957. *Separate Church & State Now.* New York: R. R. Smith.

Deane, Herbert A. 1973. 'Classical and Christian Political Thought'. *Political Theory* 1:415–26.

De La Croix, Horst and Richard G. Tansey. 1975. *Gardiner's Art through the Ages,* 6th edn. New York: Harcourt Brace Jovanovich.

Delacroix, Jacques. 1995. 'Review of "Religion and Economic Action" by Kurt Samuelsson'. *Journal for the Scientific Study of Religion* 34:126–7.

Delacroix, Jacques and François Nielsen. 2001. 'The Beloved Myth: Protestantism and the Rise of Industrial Capitalism in Nineteenth Century Europe'. *Social Forces* 80:509–53.

Delbrück, Hans. 1982. *History of the Art of War*, vol. 3: *The Middle Ages*. Lincoln, NE: University of Nebraska Press.

Dempsey, Bernard W. 1943. *Interest and Usury*. Washington, DC: American Council on Public Affairs.

de Roover, Raymond. 1946. 'The Medici Bank Financial and Commercial Operations'. *Journal of Economic History* 6:153–72.

de Roover, Raymond. 1958. 'The Concept of the Just Price'. *Journal of Economic History* 18:418–34.

de Roover, Raymond. 1963. 'The Organization of Trade'. In M. M. Postan, E. E. Rich and Edward Miller (eds), *The Cambridge Economic History of Europe*, vol. 3, 42–118. Cambridge: Cambridge University Press.

DeVries, Kelly, ed. 2010. *Medieval Warfare 1300–1500*. New York: Routledge.

Dickens, A. G. 1991. *The English Reformation*. University Park, PA: Pennsylvania State University Press.

Dixon, C. Scott. 2012. *Contesting the Reformation*. Oxford: Wiley-Blackwell.

Drogus, Carol Ann. 1995. 'Review: The Rise and Decline of Liberation Theology: Churches, Faith, and Political Change in Latin America'. *Comparative Politics* 27:465–77.

Duby, Georges. 1974. *The Chivalrous Society*. Berkeley, CA: University of California Press.

Duffy, Eamon. 1987. 'The Late Middle Ages: Vitality or Decline?' In Henry Chadwick and G. R. Evans (eds), *Atlas of the Christian Church*, 86–95. New York: Facts on File.

Duffy, Eamon. 1992. *Stripping the Altars*. New Haven, CT: Yale University Press.

Durant, Will. 1957. *The Reformation*. New York: Simon & Schuster.

Durkheim, Émile. [1897] 1951. *Suicide*. Glencoe, IL: The Free Press.

Eberstadt, Nicholas and Apoorva Shah. 2012. 'Fertility Decline in the Muslim World'. *Policy Review* 173 (1 June).

Eidberg, Peder A. 1995. 'Norwegian Free Churches and Religious Liberty: A History'. *Journal of Church and State* 37:869–84.

Eisenstadt, Shmuel N. (ed.). 1968. *The Protestant Ethic and Modernization*. New York: Basic Books.

Ekman, Ernst. 1957. 'The Danish Royal Law of 1665'. *Journal of Modern History* 2:102–7.

Encarnatión, Omar. 2013. 'The Catholic Crisis in Latin America: Even an Argentine Pope Can't Save the Church'. *Foreign Affairs*, 19 March.

Evera, Stephen van. 1994. 'Hypotheses on Nationalism and War'. *International Security* 18:5–39.

Farmer, David L. 1991. 'Marketing the Produce of the Countryside, 1200–1500'. In Edward Miller (ed.), *The Agrarian History of England and Wales*, vol. 3: *1348–1500*, 324–58. Cambridge: Cambridge University Press.

Field, Clive D. 2008. 'A Shilling for Queen Elizabeth: The Era of State Regulation of Church Attendance in England, 1552–1969'. *Journal of Church and State* 50:213–53.

Finke, Roger and Rodney Stark. 1992. *The Churching of America, 1776–1990*. New Brunswick, NJ: Rutgers University Press.

Frejka, Tomas and Charles F. Westoff. 2008. 'Religion, Religiousness and Fertility in the US and in Europe'. *European Journal of Population* 24:5–31.

Freston, Paul. 2008. *Evangelical Christianity and Democracy in Latin America*. Oxford: Oxford University Press.

Fryde, E. B. 1963. 'Public Credit with Special Reference to North-Western Europe'. In M. M. Postan, E. E. Rich and Edward Miller (eds), *The Cambridge Economic History of Europe*, vol. 3, 430–553. Cambridge: Cambridge University Press.

Garret, Brian. 2011. 'The Life and Work of Nehemiah Grew'. *The Public Domain Review*. <http://publicdomaninreview.org/2011/03/01/the-life-and-work-of-nehemiah-grew/>.

Gascoigne, John. 1990. 'A Reappraisal of the Role of the Universities in the Scientific Revolution'. In David C. Lindberg and Robert S. Westman (eds), *Reappraisals of the Scientific Revolution*, 207–60. Cambridge: Cambridge University Press.

Gee, Henry and William John Hardy (eds). 1896. *Documents Illustrative of English Church History*. New York: Macmillan.

Geertz, Clifford. 1966. 'Religion as a Cultural System'. In Michael Banton (ed.), *Anthropological Approaches to the Study of Religion*, 1–46. London: Tavistock Publications.

Gies, Joseph and Frances Gies. 1969. *Leonard of Pisa and the New Mathematics of the Middle Ages*. New York: Crowell.

Gilchrist, John. 1969. *The Church and Economic Activities in the Middle Ages*. New York: St Martin's Press.

Gill, Anthony. 1998. *Rendering unto Caesar: The Catholic Church and the State in Latin America*. Chicago, IL: University of Chicago Press.

Gimpel, Jean. 1976. *The Medieval Machine: The Industrial Revolution of the Middle Ages*. New York: Penguin.

Glock, Charles Y. and Rodney Stark. 1966. *Christian Beliefs and Anti-Semitism*. New York: Harper & Row.

Gooren, Henri. 2002. 'Catholic and Non-Catholic Theologies of Liberation: Poverty, Self-Improvement, and Ethics among Small-Scale Entrepreneurs in a Guatemala City'. *Journal for the Scientific Study of Religion* 41:29–45.

Grant, Edward. 1984. 'Science and the Medieval University'. In James Kittleson and Pamela J. Transue (eds), *Rebirth, Reform, and Resilience: Universities in Transition, 1300–1700*. Columbus, OH: Ohio State University Press.

Greengrass. Mark. 2014. *Christendom Destroyed: Europe 1517–1648*. New York: Penguin.

Gregory, Brad S. 2012. *The Unintended Reformation: How a Religious Revolution Secularized Society*. Cambridge, MA: Harvard University Press.

Grell, Ole Peter (ed.). 1995. *The Scandinavian Reformation*. Cambridge: Cambridge University Press.

Grell, Ole Peter. 1996. 'Introduction'. In Ole Peter Grell and Bob Scribner (eds), *Tolerance and Intolerance in the European Reformation*, 1–12. Cambridge: Cambridge University Press.

Grell, Ole Pater and Bob Scribner (eds). 1996. *Tolerance and Intolerance in the European Reformation.* Cambridge: Cambridge University Press.

Gribbin, John. 2005. *The Fellowship: Gilbert, Bacon, Harvey, Wren, Newton, and the Story of a Scientific Revolution.* New York: The Overlook Press.

Grim, Brian J. and Roger Finke. 2006. 'International Religion Indexes'. *Interdisciplinary Journal for Research on Religion* 2:1–40.

Gritsch, Eric W. 2012. *Martin Luther's Anti-Semitism.* Grand Rapids, MI: Eerdmans.

Guerry, André-Michel. [1833] 2002. *Essay on the Moral Statistics of France.* Lewiston, NY: The Edwin Mellen Press.

Hamberg, Eva M. and Thorleif Pettersson. 1994. 'The Religious Market: Denominational Competition and Religious Participation in Contemporary Sweden'. *Journal for the Scientific Study of Religion* 33:205–16.

Hamberg, Eva M. and Thorleif Pettersson. 1997. 'Short-Term Changes in Religious Supply and Church Attendance in Contemporary Sweden'. *Research in the Scientific Study of Religion* 8:35–51.

Haskins, Charles Homer. [1923] 2002. *The Rise of Universities.* New Brunswick, NJ: Transaction.

Hay, Denys. 1977. *The Church in Italy in the Fifteenth Century.* Cambridge: Cambridge University Press.

Hayes, Carlton J. 1917. *Political and Social History of Modern Europe.* (2 vols). New York: Macmillan.

Hayes, Carlton J. [1960] 2016. *Nationalism: A Religion.* New Brunswick, NJ: Transaction.

Headley, John M. 1987. 'Luther and the Problem of Secularization'. *Journal of the American Academy of Religion* 55:21–37.

Heal, Bridget and Ole Peter Grell (eds). 2008. *The Impact of the European Reformation.* Aldershot: Ashgate.

Hechter, Michael. 2000. *Containing Nationalism.* Oxford: Oxford University Press.

Hendrix, Scott. 2000. 'Rerooting the Faith: The Reformation as Re-Christianization'. *Church History* 69:558–77.

Herlihy, David. 1957. 'Church Property on the European Continent, 701–1200'. *Speculum* 18:89–113.

Hewitt, W. E. 1991. *Base Communities and Social Change in Brazil.* Lincoln, NE: University of Nebraska Press.

Hickey, Anne Ewing. 1987. *Women of the Roman Aristocracy in Christian Monastics.* Ann Arbor, MI: UMI Research Press.

Hill, Christopher. 1967. 'Puritanism, Capitalism, and the Scientific Revolution'. *Past & Present* 29:88–97.

Hillerbrand, Hans J. 2003. *Encyclopedia of Protestantism,* 4 vols. New York: Routledge.

Hilton, Walter. 1985. *Toward a Perfect Love.* Portland, OR: Multnomah Press.

Himmelfarb, Gertrude. 1993. 'The Dark and Bloody Crossroads: Where Nationalism and Religion Meet'. *The National Interest* 32:53–61.

Hunt, Edwin S. 1994. *The Medieval Super-Companies.* Cambridge: Cambridge University Press.

Hunt, Edwin S. and James M. Murray. 1999. *A History of Business in Medieval Europe, 1200–1500.* Cambridge: Cambridge University Press.

Hunter, Leslie Stannard (ed.). 1965. *Scandinavian Churches.* London: Faber & Faber.

Hutchinson, John and Anthony D. Smith (eds). 1994. *Nationalism: An Oxford Reader.* Oxford: Oxford University Press.

Iannaccone, Laurence R. 1991. 'The Consequences of Religious Market Structure'. *Rationality and Society* 3:156–77.

Jaki, Stanley L. 1986. *Science and Creation.* Edinburgh: Scottish Academic Press.

Jaki, Stanley L. 2000. *The Savior of Science.* Grand Rapids, MI: Eerdmans.

Janin, Hunt. 2008. *The University in Medieval Life, 1170–1499.* Jefferson, NC: McFarland.

Jenkins, Philip. 2002. *The Next Christendom: The Coming of Global Christianity.* New York: Oxford University Press.

Jenkins, Philip. 2003. *The New Anti-Catholicism: The Last Acceptable Prejudice.* New York: Oxford University Press.

Jenkins, Philip. 2006. *The New Faces of Christianity*. New York: Oxford University Press.

Jessup, David Eric. 2010. 'The Language of Religious Liberty in the Swedish Constitution of 1809'. *Scandinavian Studies* 82:159–82.

Johnson, Barclay D. 1965. 'Durkheim's One Cause of Suicide'. *American Sociological Review* 30: 875–86.

Johnson, Paul. 1976. *A History of Christianity*. New York: Atheneum.

Johnson, Paul. 2003. *Art: A New History*. New York: HarperCollins.

Jones, E. L. 1987. *The European Miracle*, 2nd edn. Cambridge: Cambridge University Press.

Jünger, Ernst. [1920] 1961. *Storm of Steel*. New York: Penguin Classics.

Kaelber, Lutz. 1998. *Schools of Asceticism*. University Park, PA: Pennsylvania State University Press.

Kearney, H. F. 1964. 'Puritanism, Capitalism and the Scientific Revolution'. *Past & Present* 28:81–101.

King, Peter. 1999. *Western Monasticism*. Kalamazoo, MI: Cistercian Publications.

Kistner, W. 1976. 'The Reformation and the Roots of German Nationalism'. *Theoria* 46:61–76.

Kittleson, James. 1986. *Luther the Reformer*. Minneapolis, MN: Augsburg Fortress.

Klaiber, Jeffrey L. 1970. 'Pentecostal Breakthrough'. *America* 122:99–102.

Kocher, Paul H. 1953. *Science and Religion in Elizabethan England*. San Marino, CA: The Huntington Library.

Kohn, Hans. 1950. 'Romanticism and the Rise of German Nationalism'. *Review of Politics* 12:443–72.

Laelber, Lutz. 1998. *Schools of Asceticism*. University Park, PA: Pennsylvania State University Press.

Landes, David S. 1994. 'What Room for Accident in History? Explaining Big Changes by Small Events'. *The Economic History Review* 47:637–56.

Latourette, Kenneth Scott. 1975. *A History of Christianity*, vol. 2. San Francisco, CA: HarperSanFrancisco.

Laurentin, René. 1977. *Catholic Pentecostalism*. Garden City, NY: Doubleday.

Lindberg, Carter. 2010. *The European Reformations*, 2nd edn. Chichester: John Wiley.

Lindberg, David C. 1992. *The Beginnings of Western Science*. Chicago, IL: University of Chicago Press.

Lindberg, David C. and Robert S. Westman (eds). 1990. *Reappraisals of the Scientific Revolution*. Cambridge: Cambridge University Press.

Little, Lester K. 1978. *Religious Poverty and the Profit Economy in Medieval Europe*. Ithaca, NY: Cornell University Press.

Lloyd, T. H. 1982. *Alien Merchants in England in the High Middle Ages*. New York: St Martin's Press.

Loane, M. [1906] 2012. *The Queen's Poor: Life as They Find It in Town and Country*. Ulan Press (location unknown).

Lodberg, Peter. 1989. 'The Churches in Denmark'. In Peter Brierley (ed.), *Danish Christian Handbook*, 6–8. London: MARC Europe.

Lopez, Robert S. 1952. 'The Trade of Medieval Europe: The South'. In M. M. Postan, E. E. Rich and Edward Miller (eds), *The Cambridge Economic History of Europe*, vol. 2, 25–354. Cambridge: Cambridge University Press.

Lopez, Robert S. 1976. *The Commercial Revolution of the Middle Ages, 950–1350*. Cambridge: Cambridge University Press.

Lukes, Steven. 1971. 'The Meanings of "Individualism"'. *Journal of the History of Ideas* 32:45–66.

McClelland, David C. 1961. *The Achieving Society*. New York: Van Nostrand.

McCloskey, Deirdre N. 2010. *Bourgeois Dignity: Why Economics Can't Explain the Modern World*. Chicago, IL: University of Chicago Press.

MacCulloch, Diarmaid. 2004. *The Reformation*. New York: Viking.

Macfarlane, Alan. 1978a. 'The Origins of English Individualism: Some Surprises'. *Theory and Society* 6:255–77.

Macfarlane, Alan. 1978b. *The Origins of English Individualism*. Oxford: Blackwell.

McGrath, Alister E. 2007. *Christianity's Dangerous Idea*. San Francisco, CA: HarperOne.

Manchester, William. 1993. *A World Lit Only by Fire*. New York: Little, Brown.

Mansfield, Patti Gallagher. 1992. *As by a New Pentecost: The Dramatic Beginning of the Catholic Charismatic Renewal*. Lancashire, UK: Proclaim! Publications.

Maritain, Jacques. 1950. *Three Reformers*. New York: Scribner's.

Mariz, Cecilia. 1994. *Coping with Poverty: Pentecostal Churches and the Christian Base Communities in Brazil*. Philadelphia, PA: Temple University Press.

Marshall, Peter. 2009. '(Re)defining the English Reformation'. *Journal of British Studies* 48:564–86.

Martin, David. 1990. *Tongues of Fire: The Explosion of Protestantism in Latin America*. Oxford: Blackwell.

Martin, David. 2002. *Pentecostalism: The World Their Parish*. Oxford: Blackwell.

Marty, Martin. 1993. 'Luther's Living Legacy'. *Christian History* 39:51–3.

Mason, Stephen F. 1950. 'Some Historical Roots of the Scientific Revolution'. *Science & Society* 14:237–64.

Mason, Stephen F. 1962. *A History of the Sciences*, rev. edn. New York: Macmillan.

Mayr-Harting, Henry. 1993. 'The West: The Age of Conversion (700–1050)'. In John MacManners (ed.), *The Oxford History of Christianity*, 101–29. Oxford: Oxford University Press.

Mecham, John Lloyd. [1934] 1966. *Church and State in Latin America*. Chapel Hill, NC: University of North Carolina Press.

Merton, Robert K. 1938. 'Science, Technology and Society in Seventeenth-Century England'. *Osiris* 4:360–632.

Merton, Robert K. 1967. *On Theoretical Sociology*. New York: The Free Press.

Merton, Robert K. 1984. 'The Fallacy of the Latest Word: The Case for "Pietism and Science"'. *American Journal of Sociology* 89:1091–1121.

Michaud, J. F. 1855. *The History of the Crusades*. New York: Redfield.

Minkov, Michael and Geert Hofstede. 2012. 'Is National Culture a Meaningful Concept?' *Cross-Cultural Research* 46:133–59.

Moeller, Bernd. 1972. *Imperial Cities and the Reformation*. Philadelphia, PA: Fortress Press.

Monod, Paul Kléber. 1999. *The Power of Kings*. New Haven, CT: Yale University Press.

Monroe, Arthur Eli. 1975. *Early Economic Thought*. New York: Gordon Press.

Monter, E. William and John Tedeschi. 1986. 'Towards a Statistical Profile of Italian Inquisitions, Sixteenth to Eighteenth Centuries'. In Gustav Henningsen and John Tedeschi (eds), *The Inquisition in Early Modern Europe: Studies on Sources and Methods*, 130–57. DeKalb, IL: Northern Illinois University Press.

Montgomery, T. S. 1979. 'Latin American Evangelicals: Oaxtepec and Beyond'. In Daniel H. Levine (ed.), *Churches and Politics in Latin America*, 87–107. Beverley Hills, CA: Sage.

Morishima, Michio. 1990. 'Ideology and Economic Activity'. *Current Sociology* 38:51–7.

Morselli, Henry. [1879] 1882. *Suicide: An Essay on Comparative Moral Statistics*. New York: Appleton.

Murray, Alexander. 1972. 'Piety and Impiety in Thirteenth-Century Italy'. *Studies in Church History* 8:83–106.

Nash, David. 2004. 'Reconnecting Religion with Social and Cultural History: Secularization's Failure as a Master Narrative'. *Cultural and Social History* 1:302–25.

Needham, Joseph. 1954. *Science and Civilization in China*, vol. 1. Cambridge: Cambridge University Press.

Needham, Joseph. 1956. *Science and Civilization in China*, vol. 2. Cambridge: Cambridge University Press.

Neitz, Mary Jo. 1987. *Charisma and Community: A Study of Religious Commitment within the Charismatic Renewal*. New Brunswick, NJ: Transaction.

Nelsen, Brent F. and James L. Guth. 2015. *Religion and the Struggle for European Union*. Georgetown, Washington, DC: Georgetown University Press.

Nelson, Benjamin. 1969. *The Idea of Usury*, 2nd edn. Chicago, IL: University of Chicago Press.

Newton, Isaac. [1687] 1971. *The Motion of Bodies* (vol. 1 of *Principia*). Berkeley, CA: University of California Press.

Niebuhr, H. Richard. 1929. *The Social Sources of Denominationalism*. New York: Henry Holt.

North, Charles M. and Carl R. Gwin. 2004. 'Religious Freedom and the Unintended Consequences of State Religion'. *Southern Economics Journal* 71:103–17.

Nuñez, Emilio A. and William D. Taylor. 1989. *Crisis in Latin America: An Evangelical Perspective*. Chicago, IL: Moody Press.

Obelkevich, James. 1976. *Religion and Rural Society*. New York: Doubleday.

O'Donovan, Oliver, and Joan Lockwood O'Donovan (eds). 1999. *A Sourcebook in Christian Political Thought*. Grand Rapids, MI: Eerdmans.

Olsen, Glenn. 1969. 'Italian Merchants and the Performance of Papal Banking Functions in the Early Thirteenth Century'. In David Herlihy, Robert S. Lopez and Vsevolod Slessarev (eds), *Economy, Society, and Government in Medieval Italy*, 43–63. Kent, OH: Kent State University Press.

Oman, Sir Charles. [1924] 1960. *History of the Art of War in the Middle Ages*. Ithaca, NY: Cornell University Press.

Ottosen, Knud. 1986. *A Short History of the Churches in Scandinavia*. Arhus: Hovedbygningen Universitet Press.

Ozment, Steven. 1975. *The Reformation in the Cities*. New Haven, CT: Yale University Press.

Ozment, Steven. 1980. *The Age of Reform 1250–1550*. New Haven, CT: Yale University Press.

Parker, Geoffrey. 1992. 'Success and Failure during the First Century of the Reformation'. *Past & Present* 136:43–82.

Payton, James R., Jr. 2010. *Getting the Reformation Wrong*. Downers Grove, IL: InterVarsity Press.

Pettersson, Thorleif. 1988. 'Swedish Church Statistics'. *Social Compass* 35:15–31.

Pettersson, Thorleif and Eva M. Hamberg. 1997. 'Denomina-
tional Pluralism and Church Membership in Contemporary
Sweden: A Longitudinal Study of the Period 1974–1995'.
Journal of Empirical Theology 10:61–78.

Picton, Hervé. 2015. *A Short History of the Church of England*.
Cambridge: Cambridge Scholars Publishing.

Pope, Whitney. 1976. *Durkheim's Suicide: A Classic Analyzed*.
Chicago, IL: University of Chicago Press.

Pope, Whitney and Nick Danigelis. 1981. 'Sociology's One Law'.
Social Forces 60:495–516.

Porges, Walter. 1946. 'The Clergy, the Poor, and the Non-
Combatants on the First Crusade'. *Speculum* 21:1–23.

Powell, Milton B. (ed.). 1967. *The Voluntary Church*. New York:
Macmillan.

Probst, Christopher J. 2012. *Demonizing the Jews: Luther and
the Protestant Church in Nazi Germany*. Bloomington, IN:
University of Indiana Press.

Rabb, Theodore K. 1965. 'Religion and the Rise of Modern
Science'. *Past & Present* 31:111–26.

Raftus, J. A. 1958. 'The Concept of the Just Price'. *Journal of
Economic History* 18:435–7.

Rashdall, Hastings. [1936] 1977. *The Universities of Europe in the
Middle Ages*, 3 vols. Oxford: Oxford University Press.

Redman, Ben Ray. 1949. *The Portable Voltaire*. New York: Penguin.

Roberts, Michael. 1968. *The Early Vasas: A History of Sweden,
1523–1611*. Cambridge: Cambridge University Press.

Robinson, Charles Henry. 1923. *History of Christian Missions*.
New York: Charles Scribner's Sons.

Rubenstein, Richard L. 1985–6. 'The Political Significance of Latin
American Liberation Theology'. *World Affairs* 148:159–67.

Rubin, Jared. 2016. *Rulers, Religion, and Riches: Why the West
Got Rich and the Middle East Did Not*. Cambridge: Cambridge
University Press.

Russell, Josiah Cox. 1958. *Late Ancient and Medieval Population*.
Philadelphia, PA: American Philosophical Society.

Russell, Josiah Cox. 1972. *Medieval Regions and Their Cities.* Bloomington, IN: Indiana University Press.

Russell, Josiah Cox. 1987. *Medieval Demography.* New York: AMS Press.

Samuelsson, Kurt. [1961] 1993. *Religion and Economic Action.* Toronto, ON: University of Toronto Press.

Sanderson, Stephen K., Seth A. Abrutyn and Kristopher R. Proctor. 2011. 'Testing the Protestant Ethic Thesis with Quantitative Historical Data: A Research Note'. *Social Forces* 89:905–11.

Schmied, Gerhard. 1996. 'American Televangelism on German TV'. *Journal of Contemporary Religion* 11:95–9.

Schrock-Jacobson, Gretchen. 2012. 'The Violent Consequences of the Nation: Nationalism and the Initiation of Interstate War'. *Journal of Conflict Resolution* 56:825–52.

Schulze, Hagen. 1996. *States, Nations and Nationalism: From the Middle Ages to the Present.* Oxford: Blackwell.

Selthoffer, Steve. 1997. 'German Government Harasses Charismatic Christians'. *Charisma* (June):22–4.

Shapin, Steven. 1996. *The Scientific Revolution.* Chicago, IL: University of Chicago Press.

Shapiro, B. J. 1968. 'Latitudinarianism and Science in Seventeenth-Century England'. *Past & Present* 40:16–41.

Shirer, William L. 1960. *The Rise and Fall of the Third Reich: A History of Nazi Germany.* New York: Simon & Schuster.

Siemon-Netto, Uwe. 1995. *The Fabricated Luther: The Rise and Fall of the Shirer Myth.* St Louis, MO: Concordia.

Siewert, John A. and Edna G. Valdez. 1997. *Mission Handbook: US and Canadian Christian Ministries Overseas,* 17th edn. Grand Rapids, MI: Zondervan.

Smith, Adam. [1776] 1981. *An Inquiry into the Nature and Causes of the Wealth of Nations,* 2 vols. Indianapolis, IN: Liberty Fund.

Smith, Christian, 1998. *American Evangelicalism.* Chicago, IL: University of Chicago Press.

So, Alvin Y. 1990. *Social Change and Development.* Los Angeles, CA: Sage.

Sorensen, Rob. 2016. *Martin Luther and the German Reformation*. London: Anthem Press.

Southern, R. W. 1970a. *Medieval Humanism and Other Studies*. New York: Harper Torchbooks.

Southern, R. W. 1970b. *Western Society and the Church in the Middle Ages*. London: Penguin.

Spong, John Shelby. 2001. *A New Christianity for a New World*. San Francisco, CA: HarperOne.

Stark, Rodney. 1992. 'Do Catholic Societies Really Exist?' *Rationality and Society* 4:261–71.

Stark, Rodney. 1998. 'Catholic Contexts: Competition, Commitment and Innovation'. *Review of Religious Research* 39:197–208.

Stark, Rodney. 2004a. *For the Glory of God: How Monotheism Led to Reformations, Science, Witch-Hunts and the End of Slavery*. Princeton, NJ: Princeton University Press.

Stark, Rodney. 2004b. 'Upper-Class Asceticism: Social Origins of Ascetic Movements and Medieval Saints'. *Review of Religious Research* 45:5–19.

Stark, Rodney. 2008. *What Americans Really Believe*. Waco, TX: Baylor University Press.

Stark, Rodney. 2014. *How the West Won: The Neglected Story of Modernity*. Wilmington, DE: ISI Books.

Stark, Rodney. 2015. *The Triumph of Faith*. Wilmington, DE: ISI Books.

Stark, Rodney. 2016. *Bearing False Witness: Debunking Centuries of Anti-Catholic History*. West Conshohocken, PA: Templeton Press.

Stark, Rodney and William Sims Bainbridge. 1996. *Religion, Deviance, and Social Control*. New York: Routledge.

Stark, Rodney, Daniel P. Doyle and Jesse Lynn Rushing, 1983. 'Beyond Durkheim: Religion and Suicide'. *Journal for the Scientific Study of Religion* 22:120–31.

Stark, Rodney and Roger Finke. 2000. 'Catholic Religious Vocations: Decline and Revival'. *Review of Religious Research* 42:5–25.

Stark, Rodney and Charles Y. Glock. 1968. *American Piety*. Berkeley, CA: University of California Press.

Bibliography

Stark, Rodney and Buster G. Smith. 2010. 'Conversion to Latin American Protestantism and the Case for Religious Motivation'. *Interdisciplinary Journal of Research on Religion* 6, Article 7. <www.religjournal.com.>.

Steigmann-Gall, Richard. 2000. 'Apostasy or Religiosity? The Cultural Meanings of the Protestant Vote for Hitler'. *Social History* 25:267–84.

Steigmann-Gall, Richard. 2003. *The Holy Reich: Nazi Conceptions of Christianity*. Cambridge: Cambridge University Press.

Stoll, David. 1990. *Is Latin America Turning Protestant?* Berkeley, CA: University of California Press.

Stoll, David. 1993. 'Introduction'. In Virginia Garrard-Burnett and David Stoll (eds), *Rethinking Protestantism in Latin America*, 1–19. Philadelphia, PA: Temple University Press.

Stone, Lawrence. 1964. 'The Educational Revolution in England, 1560–1640'. *Past & Present* 28:41–80.

Stone, Lawrence. 1972. *The Causes of the English Revolution*. New York: Harper & Row.

Strauss, Gerald. 1975. 'Success and Failure in the German Reformation'. *Past & Present* 67:30–63.

Strauss, Gerald. 1978. *Luther's House of Learning*. Baltimore, MD: Johns Hopkins University Press.

Taylor, Charles. 2007. *The Secular Age*. Cambridge, MA: Harvard University Press.

Thomas, Keith. 1971. *Religion and the Decline of Magic*. New York: Oxford University Press.

Thorner, Isador, 1952. 'Ascetic Protestantism and the Development of Science and Technology'. *American Journal of Sociology* 58:25–33.

Tomasson, Richard E. 1980. *Iceland*. Minneapolis, MN: University of Minnesota Press.

Tracy, James D. 1999. *Europe's Reformations, 1450–1650*. Lanham, MD: Rowman & Littlefield.

Trevor-Roper, H. R. [1969] 2001. *The Crisis of the Seventeenth Century: Religion, the Reformation, and Social Change*. Indianapolis, IN: Liberty Fund.

Upton, A. F. 1990. 'Sweden'. In John Miller (ed.), *Absolutism in Seventeenth-Century Europe*, 99–121. London: Macmillan.

Viereck, Peter. 1953. *Shame and Glory of the Intellectuals*. Boston, MA: Beacon Press.

Viola, Frank. 2015. 'Shocking Beliefs of John Calvin'. *Patheos*, 8 April. <http://www.patheos.com/blogs/frankviola/shocking beliefsofjohncalvin/>.

Walsham, Alexandra. 2008. 'The Reformation and "The Disenchantment of the World" Reassessed'. *Historical Journal* 51:497–528.

Walzer, Michael. 1965. *The Revolution of the Saints*. Cambridge, MA: Harvard University Press.

Weber, Max. [1904–5] 1992. *The Protestant Ethic and the Spirit of Capitalism*. London and New York: Routledge.

Welliver, Dotsey and Minnette Northcutt. 2004. *Mission Handbook, 2004–2006*. Wheaton, IL: EMIS.

Westfall, Richard S. 1971. *The Construction of Modern Science*. New York: Wiley.

Whitehead, Alfred North. [1925] 1967. *Science and the Modern World*. New York: The Free Press.

Whitehead, Alfred North. [1929] 1979. *Process and Reality*. New York: The Free Press.

Williams, Sarah. 1999. *Religious Belief and Popular Culture in Southwark, c.1880–1939*. Oxford: Oxford University Press.

Wilson, Derek. 2008. *Out of the Storm: The Life and Legacy of Martin Luther*. New York: Macmillan.

Woodward, G. W. O. 1974. *The Dissolution of the Monasteries*. London: Pitkin Pictorials.

Woolston, Thomas. 1735. *Works of Thomas Woolston*. London: J. Roberts.

Wuthnow, Robert. 1989. *Communities of Discourse*. Cambridge, MA: Harvard University Press.

Zagorin, Perez. 2003. *How the Idea of Religious Toleration Came to the West*. Princeton, NJ: Princeton University Press.

Zimdars-Swartz, Sandra L. 1991. *Encountering Mary*. Princeton, NJ: Princeton University Press.

Index

Index

Index

Index

Index

Index